The DREAM BOATS

The Beautiful People On Their Beautiful Yachts

Nancy Holmes

A Bernard Geis Associates Book
PRENTICE-HALL, INC., ENGLEWOOD CLIFFS, NEW JERSEY

Art Director: Hal Siegel
Designer: Joan Ann Jacobus

The Dream Boats: The Beautiful People on Their Beautiful Yachts by Nancy Holmes

Copyright © 1976 by Nancy H. Holmes.

Printed in the United States of America

Prentice-Hall International, Inc., London
Prentice-Hall of Australia, Pty. Ltd., Sydney
Prentice-Hall of Canada, Ltd., Toronto
Prentice-Hall of India Private Ltd., New Delhi
Prentice-Hall of Japan, Inc., Tokyo
Prentice-Hall of Southeast Asia Pte. Ltd., Singapore

10 9 8 7 6 5 4 3 2 1

Library of Congress Cataloging in Publication Data
Holmes, Nancy
    The dream boats.

    1. Yachts and yachting—History. I. Title.
GV812.H64   797.1'2   76-22461
ISBN 0-13-219345-0

For Peter and Brooke.   I finished something.

Contents

Chapter 1	One Man's Yacht	7
Chapter 2	A Very Short History of Yachting	21
Chapter 3	The Magic of Monte Carlo	28
Chapter 4	The Med	41
Chapter 5	Christina's World	52
Chapter 6	Stavros' Great White Whale of a Yacht	64
Chapter 7	A Date With Nefertiti	73
Chapter 8	Cleopatra's Barge	84
Chapter 9	Mistress to Many Men	94
Chapter 10	The Five Hundred Thousand Dollar Joy Ride	107
Chapter 11	Even the Lifeboats Had Lifeboats	114
Chapter 12	Romance on the High Seas	126
Chapter 13	Chickens of the Sea	134
Chapter 14	A Tale of Two Sales	146
Chapter 15	Just Leave It to Charles	154
Chapter 16	The New Yachting	162
Chapter 17	Emily and the Swan	172
Chapter 18	A Dream, a Queen, and a Floating Palace	179

1
One Man's Yacht

There is no engraved invitation. The phone rings instead, and Simone Levitt's voice says, "Bill and I would love it if you could come with us for a week or ten days on *La Belle Simone* this summer. I know it's only March, but we like to schedule our guests as early as possible. We're going to pick up the yacht in London the first week in July. If I tell you sort of generally where we will be, do you think you might like to come with us for a cruise?"

"Simone, darling," you say calmly, trying to keep a shred of blasé in your voice, "I'd love to. Tell me where you will be when, and I'll join you where it's most convenient for you." You look out of the window into the cold gray of March, but you have already transported yourself to the Aegean or the Adriatic or the Mediterranean, and you've already made up your mind what to wear to dinner the first night aboard.

ONE MAN'S YACHT

Simone reels off the yacht's schedule as if it were a commuter train from Grand Central Station to Stamford. "Bill has some business in England, so we'll spend a few days in London, moored at the Tower Bridge. It should be fun, as we're planning a big luncheon aboard. The Burtons used to moor *Kalizma* there for their dogs, but we can do better than that. You know, the moon will be full, and it should be lovely going down the Thames, past Greenwich, on our way to Spain.

"We'll go to Marbella and Majorca, but first we're going to stop off in Tangier to see Yves Vidal and Charles Sevigny at York Castle. Then Sardinia for a day or so, and we may stop by in Corsica on the way to Monte Carlo. We could drop you off in Monte Carlo, or you could meet us there for the next trip, starting with Capri, the Straits of Messina, and then up the Yugoslavian Coast to Venice. Dubrovnik is divine, and we can water-ski there. And you *know* how marvelous Venice can be at that time of the year. You could meet us there, if you prefer. Then, on the next lap, we're going to the Greek islands and the Turkish coast, and Istanbul. Or, if you like, come to Istanbul and go back to Monte Carlo with us."

Like the schedule, your mind is wheeling in delightful circles. You want to do it all, of course, but you agree to meet in Athens about the middle of August. Bill Levitt's secretary in his office at Lake Success, New York, is the liaison lady. She will keep you informed in case there is a change of a day or so in the yacht's movements, and she will inform the yacht just what flight you are arriving on. It's a piece of cake. Just don't break a leg between now and then. You are going off to be a guest on a yacht that is 255 feet long, cost $8 million to build, costs close to a million dollars a year to operate, carries a quarter of a million dollars in spare parts at all times, and runs an annual bill of $3,200 in light bulbs alone. Would you really want to own a yacht? Maybe not—but isn't it great to be invited?

The plane lands in Athens, and, after you pass through customs, a handsome, tanned member of the crew finds you instantly. His white tee shirt has *La Belle Simone* written on it in small block letters, like a mariner's tee shirt on any yacht, anywhere. The lettering is brown, however, as the Levitts chose brown over the more conventional blue for their yachting colors. *La Belle Simone*'s stack is bound with a wide brown stripe, and brown keeps popping up even in small details like the yacht's notepaper and cards, which are printed in brown on soft beige. Naturally, there are brown felt-tip pens provided by the dozen.

Your baggage is claimed for you, and another member of the crew, driving one of those cars that the Levitts rent in every port to provide shore transport, whisks you away to Vouliagmeni, half an hour down the coast from Athens. On the way, you indulge in a little gossip just to catch up on *La Belle* and her summer guests. *La Belle Simone*'s crew numbers between twenty-five and thirty, most of them British. You learn that the Gregory Pecks have left that morning and that Dr. Manuel Machado de Macedo, the only heart-transplant surgeon in Portugal, has arrived with his gorgeous English wife, Jackie. Everyone is having lunch at Vouliagmeni's Sea-Terrace restaurant at the moment while waiting for you and the Robert Schulers. Pat Schuler is former Metropolitan Opera star Patrice Munsel.

When you arrive at Vouliagmeni, Simone Levitt's smile lights up when she sees you, and that smile is warmer than the summer day. She is a truly beautiful woman, with a bright and generous nature. Simone is French, and, although she has three grown daughters by her first husband, she still looks like a slip of a girl. She loves to sing, she loves to dance, she loves the yacht Mr. Levitt named after her, and she loves life. Most of all, she loves her husband — and it shows.

Bill Levitt is just as busy as Simone telling you how glad he is to see you, and you are overwhelmed with the kindness of two people you not only like, but who also happen to have a huge, multimillion-dollar yacht that you are about to board and become a part of.

Our host, William J. Levitt, has a fortune based on all those zillions of houses, known as Levittowns, that sprang up all over the country after the Second World War. A forceful, dapper man in his latish sixties, Bill has a gravelly voice, a driving enthusiasm, and a love of life that endears him to his friends, who are legion. He's had yachts before (two) and wives before (two), but with his third wife and his third yacht, he hit the jackpot he had hoped for.

Simone, as in *La Belle Simone,* is a warmly pretty Frenchwoman with no particular social background. She and her first husband, Barney Korshin, had an art gallery in Rome and knew Bill Levitt and wife Number Two quite well. Bill fancied Simone for years before he worked up the courage to pop the question, which was not "Will you marry me?" but "Will you divorce for me?" Simone did both. She hasn't minded one bit having a wealthy, charming new husband or having one of the largest and most beautiful yachts in the world named for her. Proof of Bill's pudding is that even Barney Korshin likes him, and you are just as apt to run into Barney Korshin on *La Belle Simone* as not. Lucky Barney. He doesn't have the expense of either of the Simones — and they are both expensive to a fault.

§

The day is fine and, as you look out over the turquoise bay, you are suddenly in another world — the world of *La Belle Simone.* There she lies, white and gleaming, in the blue water against the blue sky. You wish lunch were over. You want to *go, go,* as quickly as possible, into the escape of the world of yachting, way away from it all.

Little boats buzz excitedly around the big yacht, and you understand their excitement. Pretty girls in bikinis, young men with slim waistlines and pocketbooks to match, flash by on mono-skis, waving and smiling at anyone aboard whose attention they can capture. *La Belle Simone* is the biggest fish in the sea, that day at least. To-morrow there will be other yachts, but today who knows? You just might be invited aboard. You can dream, can't you? They do dream, that friendly little group of hopeful sucker fish. The boldest of the lot have been known to slam a small boat into the hull of a yacht to gain attention, or vengeance, or to call out and insist noisily that they must come aboard with an important message for what-exactly-is-the-name-of-the-owner? Oh yes, Mr. Revitz, we met him in Ischia and he told us to be sure to come aboard if we ever ran into him again. Sure he did.

At last you are on the launch, and in a few minutes you'll be on board *La Belle Simone*. As you draw alongside, a crew member helps you up the ladder stairway to the deck. Waiting to greet you is one of the handsomest men on the high seas, Captain Klaus Gotsch. The captain greets all new arrivals just as tenderly as he bids them farewell ten days or so later. He has spent more than a dozen years with Bill Levitt, and he has been a man of the sea all his life. He was captain on *Les Amis*, Bill's former yacht, and went all the way through every stage of the two years' planning and building of *La Belle Simone* in Carrara, Italy. He was also in the German submarine service during the Second World War. It's interesting to observe the relationship of two men of different faiths, incomes, nationalities, and attitudes, who have come together through their mutual love of the sea. Bill Levitt was in the Seabees during the war, and as fast as Klaus Gotsch was knocking things down with his torpedoes for Germany, Bill Levitt was building things up and helping to secure the Pacific Islands for America, almost before the Marines had fired the final shots. There's a close personal friendship between the two men, and a very apparent mutual respect.

Your bags have already been unpacked below, so Bill Levitt takes you around and introduces you to his yacht. He has referred to her as his floating palace, his Taj Mahal, and his home away from home, but *La Belle Simone* is really his ultimate compliment to his beautiful wife, as well as the greatest status symbol a man can ever own.

The social heartbeat and gathering place is the Café du Ciel bar on the upper aft deck. If you've been aboard before, it's old home week, and if you haven't, the ropes are quickly learned. Ryan, the chief steward, attends to your needs or problems. He and Frank, the topaz-eyed bartender, were both successfully shanghaied by Bill Levitt from Cunard Lines. Frank's only difficulty in adjusting to life on a private yacht was learning to settle for making drinks for ten instead of four hundred. He adjusted, and happily.

Each yacht has its own set of rules. On *La Belle Simone* there are really only three: show up in time for lunch, be there for dinner, and try not to beat the host at gin or backgammon. (That's not exactly a rule, but Bill Levitt is a volatile man and the noises that emanate from a losing game have been known to intimidate even the hardiest of guests.) If you want breakfast in bed, fine. If you want to spend time on the bridge or in the chart room, fine. If you want to sleep until noon, lie in the sun all afternoon while cruising, drink until dawn, or sneak out of the film at night and bed down at ten, fine. But if you're looking for fun and if you can sing, or play the fiddle, or dance like Fred Astaire, then you're really in for a ball.

Suddenly and silently, the yacht begins to move. You sit, sipping a drink, watching the shore become small and the sea vast. You are finally away, way away from it all.

§

There are three double guest cabins below and one on the top deck, and when you step into yours, you not only find your toothbrush in the right place, you also find that your door has a golden plaque with your name etched on it. You feel right at home. It's funny how fast it becomes *your* yacht.

The cabins aren't cabins at all. They're more like bedrooms that would be found in the suites of the best hotels in the world. The only nautical thing visible is a ship's clock on the wall that tells you the truth as you slip from one time zone to another. The bathrooms are wall-to-wall marble, as only Carrara can do it.

Simone Levitt is dressed by Givenchy, and she's seen to it that, in a way, you are too, for as long as you're on *La Belle*. There are two handsome toweling bathrobes in your cabin, one short and the other long—in brown and white print, of course—made especially by Givenchy for *La Belle Simone*. There are Carmen curlers, and shampoos and spray net and suntan lotions and sleeping pills and seasick pills (heaven forbid), and all those little necessities you packed so carefully and so superfluously if you were a first-timer.

There is a phone by your bed, and one of those special telephone directories that tells you how to find anything and anyone on the yacht. If you get nervous in the night about the man you left behind, you pick up the phone and the radio operator tells you how long it will take before you can talk to him, loud, clear, and free. Guests on *La Belle Simone* telephone, cable, and communicate gratis, whenever and wherever they want to. It's one of the nicest touches. There's music on an intercom system if you want it, and in the closet you find life jackets with specific instructions in case of disaster. Highly unlikely, but highly soothing to have the jacket nearby, as long as you don't have to wear it. Another nicety is the safe hidden deep within your closet. The Duchess of Argyll, when traveling to Israel on the yacht, asked first where the safe was, and then gave instructions as to the hour she wanted a hot water bottle put into her bed. On other yachts, it's one-upmanship to ask the whereabouts of the ship's safe for your fifty-carat diamonds, but on *La Belle Simone* you have your own.

Normally, when a new group comes aboard, *La Belle Simone* puts to sea as fast as possible, heading for her next port. That way, the intimacy and magnificence of the yacht come into focus immediately. Forget the nearly thirty crew members; the world becomes ten people, two of whom are host and hostess.

Life in port and cruising life are totally different, but wherever you are, morning, noon, or night, *La Belle Simone* seems to be full of wine, women, men, and song. If you categorized the yachts of the current scene, *La Belle* would win the gold ring on the merry-go-round as being the most musical yacht. Bill has two pianos, and plays both of them well. The one in the Café du Ciel is white, shiny as nail lacquer, while the other is traditional walnut and reposes in the center of the main salon. That's the Louis Seize section, which lies between the dining and library areas. If you sit at the dining table on Bill's left or Simone's right, your view down the main salon takes your eyes ninety dazzling feet from dining table to afterdeck. On a clear day, you would swear you could see Versailles in between.

Bill plays the piano with great gusto and a sure touch. Simone sings, though her performance, when in port, depends on her degree of shyness and the number of people aboard. But the Levitts never hog the scene. They scout around for at least one or two musical compadres for every cruise, if possible. If those hang-around water-skiers had only known, they might have sung themselves aboard for their supper.

§

On the first night out of Athens, dinner was early and quiet, served in the Café du Ciel. Everyone was tired. Patrice and Bob Schuler had arrived on the overnight flight from New York. Colonel C. Michael Paul had flown in from his villa in the South of France and spent the day shopping for antiques in Athens. Jackie and Manuel Machado de Macedo arrived from Lisbon. The group on each cruise becomes tightly knit in no time at all, rather like a multiple shipboard romance. Sometimes, guests come aboard in ports along the way, but the Levitts prefer to gather a completely new group every two weeks or so.

The yacht was making her way toward Patmos, having slipped past Sunion and the great Temple of Poseidon at sunset. As the group assembled for a pre-dinner drink, everyone was looking forward to the glorious blue and white havens of the isles of Greece. Dinner was served on deck and, naturally, there was a full moon. Bill Levitt gets very angry if the weather acts up when his guests have come so far to relax. One of the round tables is moved out from the Café du Ciel and seats the customary eight guests, plus Bill and Simone, perfectly. On evenings at sea, the ladies dress up in pajamas or caftans, all very informally glamorous, and the men wear blazer jackets or handsome shirts, but never ties.

When dinner was over, at just about yawning-in time, the music system gave forth a background version of

"Embraceable You." Pat Schuler threw back her head, opened her mouth, closed her eyes, and started to sing. When she cares about a song, be it "Musetta's Waltz" or "My Man," she stuns you with her voice. She cares about "Embraceable You," and she sang it with so much body and soul that our quiet evening went the way most quiet evenings go. Michael Paul quickly found his violin (Stradivarius, no less) and, as he is a former concert violinist, his accompaniment was not bad, not bad at all. Bill Levitt was at his piano (Steinway) in two seconds (not flat) and suddenly no one was tired anymore. That's the way with most quiet evenings at sea on *La Belle Simone*.

In the morning, the Levitts, who are early risers, have breakfast in the Café du Ciel. Guests split about half and half. Those who have had trays in their cabins straggle up in time for the sun, usually about eleven. Once everyone is up, if you stand at the very end of the afterdeck with your back against the rail, facing toward the bow, the guest activity on *La Belle Simone* looks like a busy Grandma Moses painting, nautical style. In your immediate foreground is a huge circular couch, covered in beige linen and loaded down with brown terry cloth pillows. The linen cushions are pie-slice shaped, and huge. It's known as the "gang-bang" couch and it holds, lies, accommodates, or however you want to put it, anywhere from twelve to thirty bodies. On mornings at sea, everyone lies there in the sun, reading and gossiping, or having a drink before lunch. Further on is the swimming pool, with its Jacuzzi hose, and there is always someone having a swim or getting some water exercise. Farther back, completing the picture, is Bill Levitt, playing backgammon in the sun.

§

It is immoral or amoral, or both, to think in terms of taking good care of yourself on a yacht. Dieting? Exercising? On a yacht? Don't be silly. Yachts are for Lucullan revelries, indulgences, and overindulgences as you glide through a shining sea. They are for eating and drinking, making merry—and hating yourself for loving every glorious self-destructive moment of it. Bring on those croissants, fresh from the morning oven, and where is that wild honey we picked up last week in Greece? Is champagne fattening? Oh well, next week, when we get back to reality, we can get back into shape.

Sure you can. But if you go cruising on *La Belle Simone* and have a couple of ounces of energy to spare, you can get into the best shape you've ever been in. Without depriving yourself of the goodies, you can come ashore glowing with health and the sense and look of well-being that go with it.

Simone Levitt walks softly and carries a big stick when she comes on deck every morning. The Givenchy or Galitzine of the night before is hung away in the closet and Simone's navy blue morning-exercise suit makes her look like a Chinese peasant in the wrong place. "Good morning," she says, beaming her great smile at you and ignoring your pancakes, as she barefoots her way past the swimming pool, heading for the back deck. There, in full view of whichever guests are up, she starts swinging that stick around like a drum majorette gone mad. Half an hour later both she and you are exhausted. But she has limbered up her body and perspired away any little indulgence of the night before while you are sitting there.

After thirty minutes of exercise, Simone is ready for her first dip in the pool. The pool is not Olympic-sized, but it's big enough for a Jacuzzi water jet that has a certain degree of authority. Not everyone can, or even wants to, go through the exercise routine. But almost everyone loves the pool and the Jacuzzi. Press a red button on the side of the pool—and stand back, Charlie. After that, you can relax with a mint tea, hot or iced, while you watch some gorgeous coast glide by.

Nothing is tackier than a hostess who puts herself on a diet and nibbles on a carrot while everyone else is sipping Senegalese. Simone Levitt's menus are planned so you can destroy yourself effectively, if you choose, or preserve yourself just as effectively. It's discipline that is required, adding a nice ingredient of will power to the trip. At lunch, starters could be an oeuf en gelée or crudités, moving on to a great platter of cold shrimp and langoustine and, always, a big salad. Masses of mayonnaise and hot rolls are available, and the fresh fruit that is served later is accompanied by cheese for the wise and ice cream and cookies for those wanton ones with a sweet tooth. Wine is served always, but you'd be surprised how delicious soda water with a slice of lemon can be in a tall frosted stem goblet, especially if you have a view of the Bosporous over the rim of the glass. At any rate, every meal includes plenty of protein, not just creamed-crab crêpes and chocolate soufflé.

But beware — the most dangerous man aboard is Hans, the Swiss pastry chef. He is not only a superb patissier; he is also an artist, and he likes his applause to be rendered with a fork. Rex Harrison, Roger Moore, and Gregory Peck were aboard for dinner one night in the south of France, and for the occasion Hans whipped up some cakes resplendent with ribbons of icing, each one with the name of one of the handsome trio's films. (Those who come aboard in Naples see Vesuvius erupting in marzipan; in Venice, you can have your Santa Maria della Salute and eat it too.)

Hans's temper matches his talent. One night when everyone came back aboard very late, the ladies went rummaging around in the galley and discovered seven or eight plain cakes in various sizes. They ate up the smallest round one. The next day Hans was on the rampage, berating the crew for stealing his cake, and threatening to quit. That small round one was to have been the top of a wedding cake he had prepared from an old German recipe that required two weeks' aging. The wedding was two days hence. The only apologies acceptable in the circumstances were conspicuous consumption of Hans's masterpieces for the remainder of the cruise.

§

Togetherness is a potential problem aboard most yachts. You know how to get away from it all, but how do you get away from one another? On *La Belle*, it's not a problem. The Levitts give you almost complete control over how you spend your time aboard the yacht, since you are expected to put in an appearance only at lunch and at dinner. Cocktails are at eight every evening, and it's so much fun to see all those familiar faces again when you've been apart all afternoon.

On an average cruise, you spend a few days at sea for each day ashore. Bill takes care of all shore excursions, though his chef's expertise usually brings everyone back to the yacht for meals. Bill makes an exception in the case of Harry's Bar in Venice and a few favorite restaurants that he's discovered, but not otherwise. Besides, there's usually a party on board in the big ports like Venice or Monte Carlo or Istanbul. On these occasions, Simone loads the yacht with fresh flowers and the best of the local music. Sometimes she asks as many as 200 aboard for a buffet, and she may invite smaller groups for seated dinners in the dining salon. Then the yacht becomes a floating villa rather than a seagoing solarium.

After one such party, the group took one of the rented cars to go gambling at Regine's in Monte Carlo. The gambling party broke up very late, and when the casino's parking attendant brought their car, Simone said, "But Bill, this is a blue car. The one we came in was brown." And Bill said, "Red, blue, brown, who can tell what color a car is this time of night?"

It was nearly four o'clock in the morning when they returned to the yacht. Two of the crew members got off their night watch at four A.M. and knowing that all guests were dead to the world that night, they decided to take a late-night look at Monte Carlo. So off they went. For about twenty yards. The Monte Carlo police, who have been deeply under the influence of Cary Grant since *To Catch a Thief*, are wildly conscientious about their job. The two crew members landed in the Monte Carlo jail for driving a stolen car. Turned out Simone was right. The parking attendant at Regine's had given them the wrong car, and an angry owner called the flics. It took Bill Levitt and the captain several hours to spring the two crew members. They vanished into the hold this time, sheepishly.

§

The maddening part about being on a yacht like *La Belle Simone* is that you get so spoiled. So quickly. You go ashore, and the minute it's known that you are from the big white million-dollar baby lying out there, you've had it. It's not that the prices zoom; it's that the smiles change. You're an automatic Big Shot and you're bound to be a rich Big Shot, too, to be on that yacht. You are assaulted and battered by jewelers, boutique owners, freeloaders, and busted titles, and you can miss seeing a lot of cathedrals that way. Also, you become part of a court, the court that surrounds the King and Queen, i.e., the owners. Everyone tries to get at you so that they can get at *them*. It's fun to feel so film-star-ish, but soon you hate the fawning, flattery, and fanny-kissing that goes with it. The whole scene is heady stuff for a neophyte guest, but you learn immediately why big yachtsmen infinitely prefer the clean, clean, blue, blue sea.

While cruising one day, Simone Levitt called to Bill from the swimming pool, asking him to bring her a drink. There are two solid gold cocktail glasses on the bar that were a present from Simone to Bill, copies of his favorite Steuben cocktail glass. One has "La Belle Simone" printed on it. The other says "Joey Vivre," which is Simone's pet name for Bill. He brought her the drink, bending down to hand it to her in the water. He looked up and said to whomever was concerned, "How many women do you know who have their husband bring them a drink in a golden goblet, in their own swimming pool, on their own yacht?" He answered his own question. "One," he said, grinning happily, and went back to the backgammon board.

§

Now you know what it's like to be a guest on a modern yacht. Other people have yachts, of course — people like

ONE MAN'S YACHT

Onassis, and Liz Taylor and Richard Burton, and Dina Merrill — and every one of them is more spectacular than the last. We'll get to their stories soon but first let's take a brief detour into the background of yachting for a bit of perspective. Simone Levitt has got it good, but Cleopatra's barge was unmatchable for sheer luxurious expense — which is what yachting is all about.

2
A Very Short History of Yachting

A yacht is a definitive statement of wealth, affluence, power and glory. Every home should have one.

Jaghtschips are what they were called originally, a singularly ugly Dutch word. But "jaghts" they were to the Dutch who used the first swift, sleek craft for the pursuit of pirates. It was almost inevitable that yachts, as the word came to be known, would soon be used for the pursuit of pleasure. For hasn't speed always been of paramount importance to the privileged classes? What's fastest is best. That's never changed, and since yachts were the fastest vessels on the sea, for a while they became the private domain of rich royals. A handful of kings and queens set the pace, and the world has followed their style ever since.

Leave it to a lady to have the first memorable vessel used for the pursuit of pleasure. Cleopatra's barge certainly couldn't have been called speedy, but it had a style of its own that inspired Shakespeare into an unforgettable word picture of what royalty at sea was all about in the third century B.C.

> *The barge she sat in, like a burnish'd throne,*
> *Burnt on the water: the poop was beaten gold;*
> *Purple the sails, so perfumed that*
> *The winds were love-sick with them: the oars were*
> *silver;*
> *Which to the tune of flutes kept stroke and made*
> *The water, which they beat, to follow faster,*
> *As amorous of their strokes.*

It would have been hard to compete with the child-queen's simple little sailing vessel and no one did for several centuries. Mind you, the galleys of Venice busily conquered the world, and state personages had state vessels (including Elizabeth I's horribly named *Rat of Wight*), but no one was doing any competitive yachting. It didn't exist. For a long time, ships were basically utilitarian, and the life of ease was strictly a landlubber's pursuit. It's a long jump from the third century B.C. in Egypt to the seventeenth century in Holland, but it was there that yachting duly established itself as a fact and a way of life. Part of that was due to the presence, in exile, of a future king of England. Charles II, before he was crowned king in 1660, lived for a few years in Holland, and there he developed a strong taste for the pleasures of *jaghtschips*. The Dutch saw to it that he was given several beautiful *jaghtschips*, and when he made his triumphant return to England, it was aboard a beautifully carved and gilded yacht that was run up for him for just such an occasion.

Charles II's love of yachts led to yacht racing as well as cruising. Both eventually became the sport of kings and led to an eternal row between racing sailors and harbor stallions—that is, power yachtsmen. Sailors, then and now, somehow can't help but think that, because they tote that barge and lift that sail, they are better than the good old boy who just wants to come aboard his own power yacht, bark a few orders at his own captain, and do nothing more than sit with a pink gin in his hand watching the sunset. That's one row that will *never* be settled.

§

Early on, there was great confusion as to just exactly what the devil a yacht *was*. You can still waste a lot of time arguing the subject, but one safe definition is that a yacht is any vessel of over twenty feet that is used for pleasure. Full stop. Go any further and you will find yourself inextricably involved in a world of sloops and ketches, yawls and barques, cruisers and steamers, and so on, ad infinitum. A yacht is a yacht is a yacht.

For a while, luxury yachting lay dormant, but in the nineteenth century the British took to it with a passion, and their leader was Victoria, their queen. Royal yachts became a must, and dear Heaven, they were splendid. Queen Victoria led the pack, having suffered through old *Victoria and Albert I* and *II* for some fifty years before *Victoria and Albert III* was launched at the turn of the century. That elegant *Victoria and Albert III* was something to be reckoned with—all 5,000 tons and 430 feet of it. Victoria loved her big new yacht, and was quite pleased with the fact that it was larger than the Russian Czar's *Standart*, which weighed only 4,344 tons, and the German Kaiser's *Hohenzollern*, which weighed barely 3,773 tons. Both monarchs were kissing cousins of Victoria, but blood runs less thickly in the realm of competitive yachting and the little queen topped them both with the biggest boat. Even *Mahroussa*, which belonged to the Khedive of Egypt, weighed a paltry 3,500 tons. They sure knew how to build them big in those days.

In the affluent days of Empire, millionaires were a dime a dozen and yachts became a must for an earl as well as a king. America, once the Civil War ended, was generating some vast fortunes and beginning to think about catching up with the rest of the yachting world. Oddly enough, the very first yacht built in the United States was built way back in 1817 by an eccentric New England millionaire whose name was George Crowninshield. He named her *Cleopatra's Barge* — and she was a doozy. The hard-working men who were so busy carving out a new republic thought Mr. Crowninshield was as mad as a hatter, and for good reason.

The Crowninshield family fortune came from privateering during the war of 1812, and they had made a bundle from contraband captured from the British. When Crowninshield *père* died, son George started spending his inheritance as if there were no tomorrow. The 100-foot-long *Cleopatra's Barge* was painted with colored zigzag stripes on her starboard side, and horizontal ribbons of red and blue and yellow on her port side. As far as his fellow-men in Salem, Massachusetts, were concerned, George was a spendthrift nut. The yacht's interior was pre-San Francisco bordello, with chairs and couches upholstered in bright red velvet, trimmed with gold lace. The saloons were festooned with chandeliers. As a final touch to all this luxe and frippery, a gloriously painted wooden Indian was planted firmly in a prominent spot on deck — so prominently that it's said an impressionable and near-sighted Frenchman in Marseilles once saluted the wooden Indian.

George took himself, *Cleopatra's Barge,* and fourteen friends on a grand tour of the Mediterranean, and during their six-month cruise he left not a port unchurned. Thousands of people came aboard in dozens of ports, and George Crowninshield had a marvelous time. It's a good thing he did, because he had been back in Salem for less than six weeks when he died of heart disease. There wasn't exactly a line forming for the right to buy *Cleopatra's Barge* so, for practical purposes, she was converted and used in the mercantile trade. Happily, she came to the attention of King Kamehameha II of the Sandwich Islands, who bought her, sight unseen, and carefully restored her to her former glory. He sailed her in Hawaiian waters for several years until she went aground on a coral reef and sank.

§

The yacht that put the United States solidly on the yachting map in 1850 was a 94-foot black schooner named

America. Built by John Cox Stevens and five of his fellow members in the fledgling New York Yacht Club, the *America* sailed to England and trounced the best that Britain had to offer. She sailed back, in possession of what was then known as the Hundred Guinea Cup and has since been known as the America's Cup. *Everyone* has tried to take that cup away from us but no one has succeeded. England's Lord Dunraven got in a snit when his yacht lost in 1895, earning himself a huge reputation for bad sportsmanship. In contrast, Sir Thomas Lipton spent thirty years and unknown millions trying to win the cup back; he failed at that but earned himself a profitable reputation for good sportsmanship in the process. The closest race ever was between America's *Intrepid* and Australia's *Gretel II* in 1970. When *Intrepid* won, helmed by William Ficker, a California architect, both Newport, Rhode Island, and Ficker's hometown of Newport Beach, California, were awash in blue and white buttons that read, "Ficker is Quicker."

Indisputably, the great and glorious years of yachting were the periods before the First World War and between the First and Second World Wars. Even the names of yachts of those days whet your whistle. In England, Lord Brassey's *Sunbeam* was reputedly the most beautiful yacht on the sea. Invitations to parties aboard Lady Yule's *Nahlin* and Sir Thomas Lipton's *Erin* were the most sought after. Sir Thomas Lipton's racing *Shamrocks* may not have won the America's Cup, but Sir Thomas and his grocery business in England were enriched by *Erin's* very being. *Erin,* poor love, became a hospital ship in World War I and was torpedoed in the Mediterranean in 1915.

Meanwhile, Astor and Morgan and Vanderbilt became the important names in American yachting. William Backhouse Astor's *Nourmahal* (which means "light of the harem") was built in 1895 by that very Mr. Astor, partially so that he could get away from his wife, *The* Mrs. Astor, and her infernal parties. In 1928 Vincent Astor built the fourth *Nourmahal* in Germany. He asked at least one lady to marry him while cruising, which she did, and he built a ramp so that President Roosevelt could come aboard comfortably. Which he did, frequently.

No backward glance at yachts and yachting can omit the name of J.P. Morgan. Without doubt, J.P. Morgan spent the happiest times of his life aboard his four *Corsairs*. As for William K. Vanderbilt, his *Valiant* was used primarily for oneupmanship. When his daughter Consuelo became engaged to the Duke of Marlborough, Vanderbilt saw to it that the British would have nothing on him when it came to yachts. *Valiant* filled the bill to perfection. The British and the Americans were in full cry.

It all slowed up, at least temporarily, with the Second World War. Import duties on yachts built outside of America were simply too prohibitive — even for a millionaire. The Seaman's Union made it virtually impossible to pay the large crews necessary to maintain a fine luxury yacht, and so they became an endangered species.

Royalty usually owned the biggest yachts during that period but, of course, there are always exceptions to the rule and there were a few privately built yachts that outshone any royal yacht. The most notable exceptions came from America; Emily Cadwallader with *Savarona III* and Marjorie Post with *Sea Cloud* lived in a fashion as royal as any queen ever did.

§

At that time, the Greeks were nowhere to be seen. Then, in 1951, Stavros Niarchos bought a breathtakingly beautiful schooner called *Vira*, which had been built by Camper & Nicholsons in England in 1927. She'd been around for years — but Stavros hadn't. He christened her *Creole*. A glimpse of her, lying at anchor in the harbor of Villefranche, cost many a man many a penny; somehow, *Creole* made it imperative for anyone looking at her to have a yacht. In 1954 Aristotle Onassis blew in to Monte Carlo with his *Christina*. And then suddenly the Greeks were the Big Men in yachting. The British were on the wane, and only a handful of Americans really gave a hoot about owning huge, expensive statements of power. With the exception of Onassis and Niarchos, the Greeks kept a low profile, although if you scratch almost any really rich Greek you will find him owning not one but several yachts. Some are fast, some slow, some large, some small, but all are expensive. In the winter, the harbor of Piraeus is the place where at least $150 million worth of Greek yachts lie safely sheltered. Every summer the Goulandris clan with their *Paloma, Eros,* or *Arjunas* rendezvous with Embericos's *El Portal* or Mavroleon's *Radiant,* and from May until October every small Greek isle is up to its ears in large Greek yachts.

§

So don't let anyone tell you that yachting is all over. It's not, and it never will be as long as there are a couple of dozen billionaires in the world who get that yachting gleam in their eyes. It may be *different,* but it's not over.

Some people these days feel so strongly about it that, to them, a single yacht is worth a dozen homes spread over the map in strategic social and business locations. Andrew Fuller of Palm Beach, Florida, and Southampton, Long Island, and New York City, and Fort Worth, Texas, moved his worldly possessions and those of his elegant wife Gerry right out of all those cities and moved themselves right onto their yacht *Gillian.* If you want to find him, just run down to the Peruvian dock in Palm Beach and yell, "Andy!" A happy man will ask you aboard his floating home for a drink.

Just as people move in and out of yachting, yachting moves in and out of phases. But it's always there. No sooner had Bill Levitt decided to sell his *La Belle Simone* than Ray Carver decided to build his *Lac II. Lac II* is only 135 feet long, but the yachts of the year *this* year still cost a ton of money— especially if you add a helicopter to the design, as Carver did.

Somewhere right now, some man is working very hard to make enough money to walk into a yacht designer's office and say, "All right, let's go. Money's no object. When can we have her in the water?" He'll do it, too. And the first place he'll take his new yacht is to Monte Carlo, where money and yachting are a state of mind—namely, pleasure. That's where *we're* going in the next chapter.

3
The Magic of Monte Carlo

The Queen Bee of the Mediterranean — or the Med, as it is known among the chic — is Monte Carlo, the undisputed capital of the sixty sensuous miles that make up the Côte d'Azur. All tales worth telling about yachts and masters, villas and villains, and the lives and deaths of the fabled few who live in the Mediterranean world, center around Monte Carlo. Yachts are sprinkled around showily in the sea near Cap Ferrat, Eden Roc, Juan les Pins, Cannes, St. Tropez, Beaulieu, and Villefranche, but Monaco is where the best of them come home to roost.

Monte Carlo! Two magic words. A sunstruck, moonstruck 388 acres where you can break the bank or go broke any night or any day. A flower-laden postage-stamp principality whose prince comes from a family that has ruled there since the thirteenth century. The home of glorious Grace Kelly, our only royal American, who, when she

28

became Her Serene Highness, Princess Grace of Monaco, showed the world what can happen if a simple American girl just waits for her prince to come. Do you realize what might have happened if she had fallen in love with Eddie Fisher? For starters, she would never have gone tootling off on Prince Rainier's yacht, *Deo Juvante*, for a honeymoon. Not that their honeymoon was any bed of roses. Poor darling Grace got so seasick that Reindeer, as the first-namers fondly call him, had to beach her like a whale for a short time in Majorca before she gathered up enough strength to go back to the Palace and don her tiara.

At Monte Carlo the blue tongue of the port licks into the land. The Alpes-Maritimes come roaring right down into the sea, dipping sheer cliffs so steeply and suddenly into the water that there is barely room for a road, much less a principality. It's a super-dramatic sight, but without the port, Monte Carlo would be just another pretty place. One of the great thrills is to make the grand entrance into the port, and that means steaming in on your own yacht, be it large or small. The harbor of Monte Carlo is like an ancient amphitheater filled with an audience that is knowledgeable, highly sophisticated, and sometimes cruel. The port is small enough to be exclusive, large enough to handle the biggest and best yachts, and just deep enough to maneuver in. But it's also crowded and so shallow that nine days out of ten someone fouls your anchor or crosses your lines. Many a four-letter word floats succinctly out over the harbor as some frustrated nouveau millionaire realizes that he is not going to get disentangled in the foreseeable future, and that he has therefore just missed lunch with the duchess he's been chasing all summer.

Monte Carlo is *the* showplace of the money and power that go hand in hand with owning a yacht. Every yachtsman feels a certain special tingle when he sails, steams, slips, or plows into the port of Monaco. Yacht owners are, one and all, absolute monarchs, and we know that there are some good kings and some bad ones. At times you find a Bligh or a Queeg, at other times you find a man who is simply status-symbol mad. Once in a while you get lucky and find a simple man who honestly enjoys the pride of ownership and adores yachting, and that's the best kind. But no matter the nature of the beast, a yachtsman always wields power over his family and his friends. You can love him or loathe him, but once you're on his yacht, you'd better love him, because you can't leave him. Occasionally, someone gets in a real huff and dives overboard, but wise yacht guests avoid scenes and they somehow understand that yachting does strange things to otherwise normal human beings. Including themselves.

Bringing a huge yacht into the harbor at Monte Carlo makes a captain's adrenaline run high whether he is the owner of the yacht or not. No matter how many times a man does it, no matter how many times the portmaster has assigned him the same space, no matter *what*, as he maneuvers his boat he knows that he has a full audience in that amphitheater, and that every move he makes is under pitiless scrutiny. The eyes have him. They watch from everywhere. From other yachts, from the quais, from the hundreds of high-rise horrors that Rainier has made so tax-freely desirable in Monaco, or from the few old villas that still hide between acres of new glass and steel. It's thrilling to watch a really big yacht moving slowly but surely in. A good captain will bring her in gently, twirl her ever so nonchalantly around in a full circle, and back her saucily into her slip. A big yacht will have less than ten inches of space left over on either side as she settles between her two port mates. It's a whiz-bang performance, and like all superstar performances, it looks so easy. If you watch a captain carefully after he has victoriously come into dock, you will see a faint glaze of perspiration on his forehead, and a telltale nervous gleam will still be in his eyes. It ain't that easy, and the thought of scraping another yacht could send any skipper straight to the nuthouse. But if you've arrived safely in the port of Monte Carlo, and are sure you are with the best people on the best yacht, the world is your pearl. Who needs an oyster?

§

The opening shots of summer in the Mediterranean are heard at Monte Carlo in May, when the Grand Prix racing drivers are working and everyone else is watching them and playing. Hard. One of the best of the yachting playboys of our Western world, and a former racing car driver himself, is an Englishman named Michael Pearson—the Honorable Michael Orlando Weetman Pearson, to be exact. Thanks to his father, Lord Cowdray, he became the richest young man in England on his twenty-first birthday, less than a decade ago. Daddy Lord had arranged for seven million pounds (something under $20 million at the time) to flow his way when he came of age, and Michael has seen to it since that it keeps flowing. He calls it work, and to be sure, *having* money means *keeping* money—and that's work. Besides, Michael stands to inherit a bundle more, plus the title, upon his father's demise.

Naturally, he has a yacht. The yacht is called *Hedonist*, which—as all you bon vivants know—is defined in almost any dictionary as "the doctrine that pleasure is the sole or chief good in life, and that moral duty is fulfilled in the gratification of pleasure-seeking instincts and disposition." Good heavens, what *else* could one possibly name a yacht? Nevertheless, Michael had a terrible time finding a name for his yacht, and eventually he went so far as to put a blind ad in the London *Times*, offering a reward of 100 pounds to whoever turned up with a winning name. Although more than a thousand people replied, it only took a moment, over a candle-lit dinner, for one of Michael's girl friends to come up with the name *Hedonist*. Maybe she felt it was her moral duty.

Michael, as you might have guessed, has a lot of girl friends. And he gives a lot of parties. Everyone's favorite is the big bash he gives aboard *Hedonist* signaling the opening of the Grand Prix weekend and the beginning of the summer's pleasures. Michael's pals are definitely a sexy, sybaritic bunch. They bring their girl friends or their wives, or both, to Michael's parties. New faces, especially pretty girls, are welcome too.

To all outward appearances, *Hedonist* is a joyride—

and she should be, for her owner is the Hugh Hefner of the high seas. The girls on board look as if they grew there, and they all "adore" Michael. The stereo blasts forth all the newest music, frequently listened to by the very singer or group who recorded it. Every current celebrity or rich young playboy knows Michael and comes to his parties. Occasionally, a visitor even gets a glimpse of the psychedelic lights in Michael's inner sanctum, smoke-filled bedroom. That visitor is usually a girl.

Underneath the devil-may-care appearance, though, Michael has put himself and *Hedonist* together meticulously. He runs the yacht with painstaking care, although the effort rarely shows, and he has projected his own image of the rich playboy to perfection. There is much more to him than meets the eye.

Michael knew and got precisely what he wanted when *Hedonist* was built by Camper & Nicholsons in 1970. Her interiors were carried out by John Sorrell and Chuck Goodwin, two talented London friends. *Hedonist* is 85 feet long, sleeps six to eight in three big double and two big single cabins, costs more than half a million dollars, and has a crew of five. Her captain, Peter Codrington, has been with Michael since *Hedonist* went into the water. The chef, Maurice, arrived one morning hot off of the late Charles Revson's *Ultima II* after a rumble of some sort. The minute Maurice was fired by Revson, he made a beeline for *Hedonist*. As Michael tells it, "He still had his chef's toque on, and I said, 'Of course I will hire you but I will have to get some new hats for you. That one you have on is too tall for my galley.' I had been watching for a first-class chef who could get along with my skipper and had some style. Maurice likes being with younger people. Right after he came to me, we pulled into a favorite cove of mine at Ibiza for a picnic and the crew immediately went ashore to set up. There is no beach, just some wonderful rocks, and there was Maurice in his chef's toque, looking ever so snobbish, barbecuing happily away. I like that sort of thing."

Besides captain and chef, *Hedonist* carries an engineer, a deckhand-steward, and a maid. (Don't you know that a whole lot of girls fight over that job every summer? "Get close to him, Clothilde, he might even marry you.") Michael's captain and engineer stay on full pay all year round, and the steward and chef are put on part-time retainer at the end of each season. That holds them through the winter—and *to* the *Hedonist*. Michael knows how to keep a good crew together.

After the opening party for racing pals in Monte Carlo, *Hedonist* spends the next two months running all over the Med. A new set of guests arrives each week. "I have a form that the captain mails out for me that tells when we will be where so friends can join me." Michael's friends are another side to his carefully casual image. They tend to have simple names like Patrick or Rollo or Jane and are introduced that way, but they always turn out to be someone like the Earl of Lichfield, who is a cousin of Queen Elizabeth, or the Earl of Denbigh. Lord Patrick and Lord Rollo, that is. Watch Jane. She may be the next Queen of England.

All those good chums of the past half-decade had best make hay while the sun shines, though, for Michael is dreaming up a new image. He got fed up a long time ago with the constant references to his money and the constant comments on his every move. The Honorable Michael Orlando Weetman Pearson is not one of those playboys who go down the drain. He's serious about his work and about his yacht. "I've pretty much had it with *Hedonist* now—not the boat, which is beautiful, but all this running around partying all summer. I started getting fed up when we had an unfortunate scene in Marbella a few years ago. Everyone went a little wild and the whole mess involved too many parties, too much wine, several broken chairs, a certain amount of pot smoking and a lot of shouting. I got as angry with Alfonso Hohenlohe as he was with me, but since he owns the place, and invited us to leave his dear old Marbella Club, we were happy to oblige. I can't be bothered with that sort of thing anymore.

"My idea of real yachting is still a sailboat, one like the *Blue Leopard*, a seventy-year-old, 110-foot boat that I love. Speed is no longer important to me. I want a sailing yacht next. Right now, I'm going through a gradual process of changing my image. The one I seem to have now needs changing."

§

Thank heavens not everyone in Monte Carlo is all that young and wild and chic and rich. Old-timers in Monte remember the elegant era of Sir Bernard Docker and his *Shemara*. The 212-foot *Shemara* was built by Camper & Nicholsons in 1938 and, besides being a large yacht with a titled owner, she became famous and even a tiny bit notorious because of her mistress, Lady Norah Docker.

Lady Docker was a renowned beauty, but she was also used to having her own way. At one of the summer galas in the Sporting Club she began sputtering because her table was not close enough to Their Serene Highnesses, Prince Rainier and Princess Grace. Norah blew her top, and when no one came running, she plucked a small Monegasque flag out of the table decorations, tore it up, threw the pieces to the ground, and stamped on them. It was not the first time that Norah had indulged in such an outburst, but it was the last time Rainier put up with it. He barred the Dockers from Monaco. For a yachtsman, being barred is the equivalent of excommunication. It means that the portmaster suddenly finds that he has no berthing space available and will have to cut off your auxiliary power plus water and telephone service. Well, the tiny environs of Monaco don't really matter all that much, but the laws of Monaco also happen to be the laws of France. The Dockers were *persona non grata* not only in Monte Carlo, but in all the ports of France.

It should have been a tempest in a teapot and forgotten by the next day, but it was not. Norah Docker took herself, her husband, and *Shemara* right over to Portofino and Capri for the rest of the summer. Fie on Monte Carlo! She should have let things cool down, though, because as glamorous as Portofino and Capri are, they are only for short visits.

And as if that weren't trouble enough, Norah slapped

an Italian customs man in a wild altercation, apparently witnessed by about fourteen thousand people, all of whom have a different version of the story. Whoosh! There went another country.

For a few summers the Dockers lurked around Spain or the north coast of Africa. They ran up and down the Adriatic, stopping off in dozens of Dalmatian islands, but Venice was closed to them, and the whole thing got too depressing for them, poor dears. Sir Bernard decided to lie low for a while, so he chartered *Shemara* out the next summer to First National Bank of Boston's Serge Semenenko. Henry Ford chartered her occasionally in July, but *Shemara* was closely associated with Serge Semenenko for many years.

Serge Semenenko is a Russian-born American citizen who became famous in both banking and the film industry by persuading the First National Bank of Boston to lend money to an ailing film industry. The result was profitable for everyone concerned, and especially for the brilliant Mr. Semenenko. An inveterate traveler, Serge preferred to take *Shemara* to Acapulco for several months in the winter and then spend the summers cruising in the Mediterranean. When Serge was not on the telephone, he was lying on the back deck of *Shemara*, soaking up the sun that he so loves, and listening with eyes closed to whatever deal was being presented to him by one business guest or another. If there's anyone who knows how to combine business and pleasure comfortably, it's Serge Semenenko.

Serge brought *Shemara* back to Monte Carlo after the exile of the Docker years, and with her he brought his gorgeous wife, Jini, and his gorgeous daughter, Christine. The Semenenkos took *Shemara* from one glittering end of the Med to the other, picking up friends in various places like Istanbul or Venice but always returning to Monte Carlo at the end of August. Everyone wanted to be invited on *Shemara*. Jini and Serge were as charming and easygoing as a host and hostess could be. Serge made only one rigid rule for his guests: No breakfast trays were to be served in guest cabins after seven P.M.! How's that for an agreeable host? He enlarged his crew from thirty to thirty-two each summer, as he wanted his night stewards on hand when he or his guests wanted anything, no matter what the hour. Many a bottle of champagne was discreetly delivered to many a cabin in the wee hours of the morning. In the Docker years, the yacht had an intercom system with the controls hidden in a huge samovar that was on a chest in the sitting room section of the master cabin. From there, one could tune in and listen to anything that was going on in any cabin. Serge Semenenko dismantled it when he was aboard. Norah might have been nosy, but the Russian-born Mr. Semenenko was not.

Every year, the Semenenkos gave the last great party of the summer, and those parties are still legend. The Semenenkos were besieged for invitations and they needed a small army to fight off the gate-crashers. Pre-party dinners were given in all the important villas and then, at about ten-thirty, the two hundred or so guests began to head for the *Shemara*. *Shemara* was dressed to the nines, laden with lights and flowers, and the music blared away from her top deck and filled the port. Champagne flowed like champagne only seems to flow in French territory. Guests fluttered about like expensive moths, ate and drank, danced and were merry until dawn. Raoul and his orchestra, from the Elephant Blanc in Paris, played every year for the Semenenko parties, heating up the night with their fabulous Cuban love songs. It wasn't a party that was easy to leave. The beautiful young daughter of the mayor of Philadelphia was invited one year, and danced like a dervish until she was too dripping wet to continue. She had no intention of leaving either the party, the music, or the handsome young men she had met, but she *had* to dry off. One of her escorts whipped her off to her hotel, where she changed her dress in two seconds flat, and back she came, ready for more, more, more.

There was all sorts of music on *Shemara*. Mrs. Deane Johnson, the first Mrs. Henry Ford, reminisces fondly about another summer's night.

"We asked a few friends aboard for dinner one night. Anne and Charlotte were young girls then. After dinner, we all sat out on deck and we noticed a lot of young men hanging around *Shemara*, gawking at us. That happened all the time, but all of these handsome young men were wearing white tie and tails. Henry went and asked them who they were. When he heard a good American accent, he invited all of them aboard for a glass of champagne. There were about fifty of them, and they turned out to be the entire Yale Glee Club. They had been invited to give a concert at the Palace that night for the Rainiers. When they finished they decided to have a look at all the yachts in the harbor. We talked to them for a while when suddenly, by some unnoticeable, invisible signal among themselves and without a word of warning, they started to sing. As long as I live, I will never forget the sound of their voices floating out over the water. The port looked so beautiful with all the yachts lit up, and everyone on every yacht was listening, just as we were. I have never heard anything lovelier and I know damn well we had a much better concert than the one at the Palace."

Serge Semenenko and Henry Ford were enjoying *Shemara* but Sir Bernard Docker and his Norah were not, so he decided to sell her. Running a yacht is trouble enough without your wife raising cain in one country after another, which does narrow your cruising range considerably. *Shemara* was sold to Harry Hyams, another English multimillionaire but one with a nice quiet wife. As it turned out, Sir Bernard Docker was still in trouble after he sold *Shemara*. Harry Hyams promptly sued him, claiming that even though *Shemara* had been sold to him for a good price, with a Lloyd's 100A1 rating, she was in awful condition. Frightful, actually. Hyams wanted to know just what Sir Bernard intended to do about it. Nothing was what Sir Bernard intended to do about it, and that's exactly what he did. The suit went on for several years, and when it was finally settled, compromises had been made on both sides. Hyams proceeded to refit *Shemara* expensively and expansively, but after all was said and done he hardly ever used her. She sits in Southampton year after year, practically abandoned. A lot of Johnny-come-lately yachtsmen get discouraged unless everything goes just right, and Harry Hyams is apparently one of those. The yachting world lost two lively ladies when *Shemara* and Norah Docker became inactive. It may never see their likes again.

§

But none of this affects Monte Carlo. Monte Carlo was, is, and always will be the place that has everything, in the sea that has everything. Monte Carlo will ever change and never change, and it will never, never be passé. All the other places are places to go; Monte Carlo, the Queen Bee, is where it all starts. Prince Rainier has created advantages that make and keep his tiny principality a practical as well as an alluring way of life. The world's biggest and best yachts, owned by the most impressive and powerful names in international society, are sheltered in the port. Most yacht owners keep a *pied-à-terre* in Monte Carlo, too, as residents of Monaco pay no corporate or personal income taxes. That statement can be made about very few countries. To realize its importance, all you have to do is look at the names of the occupants of any of the multitudinous high-rise horrors that are defacing the old, graceful Monte Carlo. Not a nationality is unrepresented. The Prince knows his business. In the casinos, the gambling purrs smoothly on, summer and winter. New hotels take up what little space still exists, most of them built on land dredged up out of the bottom of the Med and encroaching on its waters.

Monte Carlo, more than any other place along the glorious sixty-mile stretch of the Côte d'Azur, still has the most expensive jewelers, the richest banks, and *two* of the world's fairy tale hotels. One of them, the dear old Hermitage, hangs over and nestles under the railroad tracks, and many a neophyte guest has been known to rise three feet from his bed when the train comes roaring past. It sounds as if it's coming right through your room and feels like a Turkish earthquake. The Hôtel de Paris is the heartbeat of Monte Carlo. Its cavernous lobby is the clearinghouse of the entire Côte d'Azur. Everyone meets there. If you don't make an appearance at the right time at least once a summer, and if the bartender (who used to work for Onassis) doesn't know you by name when you walk into the green and gold bar, you are not part of the world of the Med. With or without a yacht.

Prince Rainier, the man who *is* Monte Carlo, is a Grimaldi, and the Grimaldi family has reigned in the principality for nine centuries. That should give a reigner an edge, but when Aristotle Onassis blew into town after the Second World War, Monaco nearly became Monte Greco. Through about thirty of his corporations, he secretly bought up controlling shares in the all-powerful Société des Bains de Mer. The Société des Bains de Mer owned the Casino, the hotels, the golf course, the theater, and therefore most of Monaco. In the beginning, Rainier was delighted to have Onassis pouring money into the war-weakened economy of Monaco, but in the end the two men were at sword points. Two was a crowd, in their case, and the battle for control went on for more than a decade.

Yachts played a major role in the feud. Onassis brought his newly converted *Christina* into Monte Carlo in 1954. Every time Rainier looked down from the palace to the port, he saw *Christina*, which was several hundred feet longer than his dear little *Deo Juvante*. *Christina* was a shimmeringly lovely sight from the outside, and larded on the inside with more exciting, powerful, and interesting guests than most of those who came up the hill to the palace. The Prince may have burned, but he didn't fiddle. He got Onassis out, bodily, at least for several years. As a result, newlywed Princess Grace never received what would have been the most breathtaking of all of her wedding presents.

Onassis had found a schooner with the lovely name of *Fantome*, which he planned to give to her. He also planned to kill two birds with one yacht. *Fantome*, as a present to the girl now princessing it over Monte Carlo, would not only put any and all other presents to shame but would also once more nick his old rival, Stavros Niarchos. Niarchos had his own exquisite schooner, *Creole*, then, and *Fantome*, equally lovely, was almost seventy feet longer than *Creole*. What a present!

The battle for power between the two men changed

everything. Onassis vanished from Monte Carlo for several years and *Fantome* never made it to Grace.

In 1967 the battle was over. Onassis was forced by a vote of the Monegasque people to sell out his interests in the Société des Bains de Mer. Rainier had won. Soon the wily Greek came back to Monte Carlo and established cordial relations with his former enemy. Both men knew very well that Monte Carlo was the supreme amphitheater of social power in the mad, mad, mad, mad world of the Med, and that it was the only place to be.

4
The Med

The Mediterranean Sea is the greatest body of water for yachting in the whole wide world. It is a watery playground of infinite variety, and no yachtsman who has ever tasted of its sybaritic pleasures would disagree. If the Med needs a slogan, it could be called "the sea that has everything."

The Med has as many lives as a cat and more faces than Eve, and all of this fabulous hullabaloo happens within a stretch of sixty miles. Between St. Tropez and San Remo alone there are two countries, one principality, all of the Côte d'Azur, and thirty ports. Just to show you how fast-moving this world is, ten years ago only the ancient ports of Monte Carlo and Cannes existed. Today the thirty ports welcome more yachts than ever before: The titled and the idle rich are no longer the only ones whose pleasure craft ply the Mediterranean.

Hollywood movie moguls have become part of the yachting life of the Med. They love the luxurious life, and to all of them (even as to you and me) a yacht is the top status symbol. Producer Sam Spiegel, one of the best-known and longest-lasting of the mogul breed, staked out a big yacht and all that goes with it the moment he made enough money to get his hands on one. Sam's name is a household word in the film industry, although for a few capricious early years he operated under the alias of S.P. Eagle. When he got rich enough to cope with a yacht, he took back his old name. Sam is one of those men who become international darlings for a reason easy to grasp. He understands people as only a mogul can. He knows that everyone in his right mind wants to meet Paul Newman, or have tea with Princess Grace, or go out with an ex-king or a future queen, be they movie or royal. Or be invited on a yacht. Sam can arrange all of those things.

That's why he got *Malahne*. After all, a yacht is a useful and desirable form of transportation. You can get away *to* something, *from* something, and *with* almost everything, if your yacht is big enough. So in 1952 Sam, who was a Med lover already, took to yachting in earnest on 165-foot *Malahne*.

Sam always has a flock of pretty girls around, and sometimes he even remembers their names. Famous actors, actresses, writers, directors, even bankers, come running when Sam invites them to cruise with him on *Malahne*. He never forgets *their* names. It's that kind of yacht.

Once, when Robert Bolt, author of *A Man for All Seasons*, arrived to spend a week, there was a pretty girl lying on the top deck sunning herself. She had a supple body, a French accent, and a deep tan. Bolt's skin was that awful, tattletale shade of white that proclaims you've been stuck in England all winter. "What a beautiful color you are," Bolt observed happily, noting that her bikini covered not more than one tenth of her body area. "Oh sank you, Robert," she replied in a sad little Gallic tone. "It is zee color of idleness."

Zat was true. She was the color of expensive idleness. All of Sam's guests on *Malahne* turn that color if their little hearts so desire. Sam sees to that. He has

42

wooed, won, intrigued, forced, begged, or bullied some of the world's better VIP's to board his yacht, and he doesn't care if they go home sea-green, as long as they leave their signatures behind, preferably on a contract but at least on the guest register. For years, *Malahne* has been a most legitimate tax deduction as well as one of the most desirable yachts afloat. Guests may laze their lives away, but Sam never stops working when he is on his big glamorous floating office. Sam is the ultimate snob, and no snob worth his sea salt has ever gone yachtless. Even multimillionaire Paris Singer, who was Isadora Duncan's love and father of one of her children, bowed to snobbism. "You have a big yacht in Cannes, don't you?" Isadora asked one day. "Can't we take a cruise on her?" "*You* can," Singer replied. "I can't. I get seasick, you know."

Sam never gets seasick, and if ever a yacht was comfortable, *Malahne* is. Sam commissioned Tessa Kennedy, one of the brightest and best young decorators in London, to keep her spruced up. *Malahne* was built by Camper & Nicholsons in 1938 and she is slow and spacious and *needs* sprucing up once in awhile. In the main salon, Tessa put down geometric carpeting, slip-covered the couches and chairs in yellows and greens, and flung around dozens of cushions made of turquoise blue and shocking pink duck cloth. She had everything made in two's, so *Malahne* is always as fresh as a daisy and if you spill a drink no one panics.

Sam rarely takes long cruises, but he invites flocks of famous friends aboard constantly. He might go off with his flock for a few days, but he hates to get too far away from Monte Carlo because he would miss all the parties, especially the ones he gives. Everyone loves to hear Sam's deep voice booming an invitation: "But darlink, you must come to *Malahne* for lunch tomorrow, just a few people, one o'clock. Vee go to the Isles of Cannes." You'd better be on time, too, because Sam never waits for anyone and he often forgets who or how many he has invited. Sam's celebrity scene is breathtaking. When Cary Grant arrives in Monte Carlo, he checks in with Sam before he calls Grace, and you know Grace who. Anyhow, it's maddening to see

the likes of Lauren Bacall, Jack Nicholson, a few Rothschilds, and the Comte de Paris slip softly out of the harbor heading for those lovely Isles of Cannes while you are
racing down the hill in a taxi, ten minutes too late. Time,
tide, Sam, and *Malahne* wait for no man.

One small, unbeatable circumstance depressed Sam
so much that he built a house in St. Tropez. He divides his
time now between *Malahne* and the new house. The reason for his depression was Stavros Niarchos. Sam always
berthed *Malahne* in Monte Carlo on the wrong side of the
tracks, so to speak, on the starboard side of the port. The
big shots of yachting all have to be in dead center or on the
right-hand side.

Not Sam. *Malahne* was parked by the warehouses
and the Riva speedboat offices, with Prince Rainier's palace
behind him and all of Monte Carlo spread out in front of
him. It was the best yacht on the "out" side until a bigger
fish slipped in, very much noticed, one day. Stavros
Niarchos chose to make a permanent berth for his gargan-
tuan new *Atlantis* right beside Sam. Sam was beside himself. *Atlantis* blocked Sam's view of everyone and everyone's view of *Malahne* more effectively than a combined
eclipse of the sun and the moon. *Malahne* is 165 feet long;
Atlantis is 380 feet long. 'Tis said, and 'tis true, that the
arrival of *Atlantis* and Niarchos sent Sam scuttling to the
house he built in St. Tropez where *no one* blocks his view.

§

The villa life of the Côte d'Azur is very important to the
yachtsmen of the Med. It's all part of the game of who has
what, and where. The beauty and proximity of three especially desirable villas make invitations to them absolute
musts for any socially acceptable yacht. The sea is the
playground of the Med. The land is a place where you cash
checks. But you must be invited to La Leopolda, high in
the hills above Ezes sur Mer, or to Villa St. Jean or La Fiorentina, both on Cap Ferrat, or you might as well take your
yacht to Algeria and forget the south of France.

Yachts poke their pretty noses out of Monte Carlo

44

harbor and come to rest in the bay of Beaulieu before eleven A.M. Sunshine and champagne are the order of the day until time for lunch with one of the four full time or part-time residents of the big three villas. When Mary Lasker or Mary Wells Lawrence or Rosemarie Marci-Rivière or Colonel C. Michael Paul open their baby blues in the morning, they reach for their binoculars — it's yacht-checking time. The great villas and the great yachts form a mutual admiration society.

La Fiorentina, for years the residence of Lady Kenmare, spreads over the entire point of Cap Ferrat. It is the jewel in the crown of a collection of homes owned by Braniff President Harding Lawrence and his equally successful wife, Mary Wells Lawrence. Old friend, Mary Lasker, rents it from them in August, and La Fiorentina is the scene, night and day, of some of the most splendid summer parties. And robberies. At one of Mary Lasker's dinners, two elegant gentlemen arrived half an hour late by speedboat and rushed up the long cypress-lined steps toward the house. Twenty minutes later they rushed back down and sped off in their Riva — with a lot of Mary Lasker's jewels in their pockets. Fortunately, the men who didn't come to dinner were caught at the Nice airport the next day.

Closer to the tiny port of St. Jean on Cap Ferrat is the Villa St. Jean, the summer home of banker Jean Pierre Marci-Rivière and his wife Rosemarie, the former Mrs. Ernest Kanzler. Villa St. Jean is a huge heap of big boulder-like rocks. It has endless rooms and broad terraces; it suited the taste of the social tigers at the turn of the century but is impossible to cope with in today's servantless world. Rosemarie got fed up with the problems of running the place but no one offered enough money to buy it, so she closed the big villa down completely and built a smaller one right on the sea at the end of her property. She still uses the terraces of dear old Villa St. Jean for her luncheons, but lives a less complicated life in her new little Villa St. Jean, Jr.

The third great villa, La Leopolda, sits supremely on the hills high above Beaulieu and Ezes. It was built for King Leopold of the Belgians, who lived there and loved it for years. Then, for a while it was owned by a Canadian multimillionaire, Izaak Walton Killam, and after that by Gianni Agnelli, chairman of Italy's Fiat. Neither of them did the villa any harm at all. Quite the opposite. Dorothy Killam added a glorious Olympic swimming pool and Gianni Agnelli provided tennis courts and a helicopter pad. La Leopolda is now the domain of Colonel C. Michael Paul. The Colonel is a white-haired, good-natured, Russian-born American who still plays the violin like the professional he once was. Colonel Paul kept a large yacht called *Seven Seas* in Palm Beach but, after the death of his wife—the wealthy Josephine Bey, who was once the American Ambassador to Norway—he sold it and bought a smaller ship, *Seven Seas, Jr.*, which he keeps in the new marina at Beaulieu. He whips down the hill from the Leopolda, jumps aboard *Seven Seas, Jr.*, and his captain dashes him off to whichever party he is invited to that night. If the good Colonel gets sleepy on the way home, he just beds down aboard and wakes up safe and sound in the marina in Beaulieu. He hosts luncheons at La Leopolda at least twice a week and gives one large party in July. The yachts can't get up his hill, but the yachters do. If you know one of the Big Three, you are in, and with everyone.

Villa owners on Cap Ferrat all have boats of their own, most of them racy Riva speedboats, used for water-skiing and getting around. David Niven is a familiar sight at his Villa Lo Scoglietto, and Gregory Peck and his French wife, Veronique, rent nearby. Baron Edmond de Rothschild, the richest Rothschild of them all, has a motor yacht, a sailing yacht, and a villa. Rex Harrison is the newest resident, having sold his longtime home in Portofino. Prince Youka Troubetskoy beds down at Villa Mayou on a cliff that hangs dizzyingly from the road level above to the sea at Ezes sur Mer, a drop of some four hundred feet. Youka has a nice big yacht but his favorite toy is a little Chinese junk. The junk is painted bright red with red sails. It shows up at all the best cocktail parties, carrying the Prince and his guests, and it is called the *F.U.*

§

Cannes is the next most popular spot on the Côte d'Azur. It's a madness at Film Festival time. The smart movie people charter yachts to get away from the noisy, mindblowing, never-ending activities of the Carlton Hotel. Kirk Kerkorian, the man who owns MGM and the MGM Grand Hotel in Las Vegas, charters *Khalidia* from the Saudi Arabian billionaire, Adnan Khashoggi, having sold it to him in the first place. (That sale is a tale in itself, which we'll get to later.) It's all very chic and very Hollywood. They show films on the yachts even when at least a thousand films are being shown in the regular, landlubber festival theaters.

There are two ports in Cannes. The Old Port is still one of the biggest and best; it services more yachts for serious repairs than any other port in the social part of the Med. The new marina is called Port Pierre Canto. Its 654 berths are more fashionable and more expensive than those in the Old Port, and it has one big fish berthed there that is the envy of a lot of current-day yachtsmen. Helmut Horten, a German department store tycoon, built *Carinthia VI*, hot on the heels of his *Carinthia V*, and for a pretty dramatic reason: *Carinthia V* sank during her maiden summer. John Bannenberg, one of the top interior designers in yachting today, had hardly gotten the curtains up on *Carinthia V* before she went pounding off to Athens. There, Helmut and his pretty wife Heidi disembarked with their guests and flew home to Vienna. It's a good thing.

Carinthia V set out for Cannes from Piraeus, and late at night as she streaked through the Ionian Sea, she struck a rock that ripped her hull to bits. She sank in sixteen minutes and although her crew was saved, *Carinthia V* was gone forever.

In no time at all, however, *Carinthia VI* came off the drawing board and went into the water and, when she is in port, she is the tourist attraction at Port Pierre Canto. Her hull is painted deep blue and she's the biggest and fastest and most expensive yacht in Cannes. *Carinthia VI*'s captain tends to avoid Corfu. As a matter of fact, she stays in Port Canto, taking short trips rather than long ones.

Another fixture in Cannes is Fritz Loewe, the man who wrote the music for *My Fair Lady* and *Gigi*, among other great hits. His yachting life was entirely different from anyone else's. Every year, Fritz took the same suite at the Carlton Hotel for the months of July and August, and chartered the same big sailing yacht for those months. For years he chartered *Giraz II*, a ninety-foot motor sailor with a crew of six. Giraz means "seagull" in German, but Fritz did very little flying *or* sailing. He gave luncheons every day.

"What would I do if I didn't have a yacht?" he asked. "My suite at the Carlton was lovely, but you cannot stay on the beach with all those dreadful people. I just go down to the beach, earlyish, and look around. You know, 'Hello, hello' if I saw a pretty girl. Or girls. When I found one, I would say, 'Would you like to come aboard my yacht for lunch?' Then the girl would look very skeptical at first, and then interested all of a sudden and she would say, '*You* have a yacht? Where?' and I would just wave my hand towards *Giraz* and say 'There.' *Giraz* looks very big sitting out there, and very beautiful. As most girls have not been on a big yacht like that, they nearly always said yes. We would go aboard. I would always take their parents or grandparents, too, if they did not want the girls to go alone.

"My captain's wife is from Holland and she is an excellent cook. I had the same marvelous lunch every day for sixteen years and I never changed the menu. God, I hated it after about six years, but now I love it again. We would never be fewer than six people. We would start with fifteen different crudités, all the best of the baby vegetables from the market, some served raw and others cooked lightly, like delicious little baby cauliflower, cooked Chinese style, or tiny carrots and haricots verts. Then we had fish or lamb or chicken as a main course, cold or broiled, but always very simple. We kept bowls of fresh fruit for dessert in the cooler box on deck, and when we would open the wine that was chilling there, we'd let some of it spill over onto the fruit for later on. But the best part of the luncheons was when we got to the cheeses. We'd start with that great white Boursault that tastes like a sixteen-year-old girl, then a Pont l'Évêque and Port Salut and

Chevres, and then finally work up to the grand, ripe Camembert that reminds me of a perfectly seasoned woman."

After lunch, *Giraz II*, if she had left port at all, went back to her slip, and Fritz returned to his suite for a nap. The girls he likes are always young, and always pretty. Some catty ladies who are too old to catch Fritz's fancy, which means over twenty, would sit under their umbrellas on the wide beach and watch every move on *Giraz II* through their binoculars. They would dutifully report all the visible activity each evening in the bar. In Cannes, it is known as "binocular gossip," and is taken for what it is worth. Fritz fooled them often by showing the girls the engine room after lunch, so not everything that happened aboard was aboveboard. To Fritz, the girls and the Med both had their charms.

§

Yachts, and the beautiful people thereon, have begun to bypass St. Tropez when meandering around the Med for a summer. Until recently, St. Tropez was one of the musts. Now it is too hot, too smelly, too small, and too crowded, and the first-raters on the big yachts stop in only for the shopping. The port is lined with boutiques and the boutiques are crammed with the best status symbol clothes. What you find in St. Tropez one summer is worn in the rest of the world the next. A certain tee shirt or belt or pair of jeans that can be found only in St. Trop becomes the uniform, and everyone has to have one or twenty. But the original charms of the small fishing village are mostly gone.

Too many small boats are anchored in the port, where the predominant aroma is garlic soup. The big yachts could never get in anyhow, and mooring outside is a hassle because a launch must be put into the water to take the yachting party in to shop and have lunch. By the time they are ready to return, the local gendarme has chased the launch and boatman away, unless some substantial francs have changed hands. There is an alarmingly commercial attitude on the part of the locals, and prices in St. Tropez are based on what the traffic will bear. The mushrooming colonies of apartments are crowded, ant-fashion, with the young or trying-to-be-young who work so hard at being with-it that they are exhausting, and you don't give a hoot if you never see any of them again. The nude beaches are full of oily nude bodies that would look much better if they were covered with some of the resort's super clothes. The bistros are packed with fish out of water, be they people or poisson. Brigitte Bardot, who put the place on the map when she built a house there a decade or so ago, is thought of as a senior citizen. Think that one over.

The yachting customs of the Med have changed in many places, not just in St. Tropez. Great big knock-down drag-out parties are pretty much a thing of the past, just as great big knock-down drag-out yachts are. Everyone still rushes off to Venice or Istanbul or Marbella or the Greek islands on their smaller, swifter craft, but hostesses in the great villas and palazzi content themselves with smaller parties now.

A number of things are responsible for the change. The rich are just as rich, but they cannot get servants. The press is scandal-mad, and the wilder doings so avidly reported about Princess So-and-So's party are frequently made up. Kidnapping and robbery have become almost routine. There seem to be thousands of new faces every summer. In the past a new face was sought after, but today that face had better arrive armed with impeccable introductions.

The parties and the yachts of the Med may be on a smaller scale than those of the good old days, but there is still something innately satisfying about having guests arrive for a party by yacht. Hostesses adore it. "The Guinnesses are coming, you know, but there isn't a decent spot left for them to berth *Sarina* . . . " worries a party-giving lady—knowing full well that Loel Guinness could push aside the entire Sixth Fleet in order to dock his yacht in the proper place. He would, too, if he and his glorious wife, Gloria, hadn't changed their habits just as the young have. The Guinnesses can, as always, be found in Sardinia for part of the summer, since Loel owns a good hunk of Sardinia, but *Sarina* cruises more than she makes port, and every summer her guest list includes the same people — the Charles Wrightsmans and the William Paleys.

In ever-diminishing numbers, the old and the old-fashioned on their old yachts still plow slowly through the sea, waited on hand and foot by their aged personal maids and valets, but that is not the life of the *jeunesse dorée* at all. Health, not hangovers, is the young yachter's bag. They streak across the water on their speedy and expensive new yachts, rendezvousing at an arranged place at an arranged time with two or three other boats. In the evenings, wherever they may be, they change into pale cotton shirts and immaculate duck pants, hot off the rack from St. Tropez. No black-tie seated dinners at sea for them. The group gathers on one or the other's boat or in the favorite bistro for simple food and a carafe of wine. They may dance all night in the local discotheque, drinking orange juice by the gallon, but the next day, brown of body and white of eye, they are off for another country.

The most tremendous of all changes in the social mores of the Med is due to the accepted sexual permissiveness of the times. The beautiful young thing of the past had parents, chaperones, and probably a crew of sixty to watch over her on Daddy's yacht. Daddy would have fallen overboard if he had known what was coming. The younger generation now have yachts of their own and they go where they damn well please. They eat, drink, sleep, and make merry wherever they like, with whomever they choose. They are basically snobbish, a wild, pretty bunch, and quite smug. They are constantly looking at themselves and thinking about themselves and gossiping about themselves, but in that way they are no different from their parents before them. Everything changes and everything stays the same.

5
Christina's World

The most famous Greek of the twentieth century was Aristotle Socrates Onassis. He made his home on a yacht called *Christina*, a yacht that more accurately might have been called *Ari*. It never belonged to a woman in any way beyond the fact that it was named for his only daughter, Christina, who now owns it. But in its heyday, it was Ari's yacht, every expensive cream-colored ton of her. He loved her, and the love affair was consummated for more than six months of every year. *Christina* was the possession that he loved most in all of his moneyed world, and the place where he kept his heart.

In his time, Onassis loved and was loved by some of the more fascinating ladies of our century, but none of them ever held a candle to *Christina*. Perhaps this was because a lady's loyalty to him was sometimes based on his generosity to her, rather than hers toward him, and was therefore suspect. All of his women were part of the game, including his first wife, Tina Livanos Onassis Blandford Niarchos, now dead, and his second and last wife, Jacqueline Bouvier Kennedy Onassis, who is a widow once more. Among others, Callas and Garbo strolled into Onassis' life over the years, and although Maria Callas certainly lasted as a "great friend," the lady whose bed Onassis always returned to was berthed in Monte Carlo, Piraeus or at the island of Skorpios, flying a Liberian flag.

The quality that set Onassis apart from most men, and from all other Greeks, was impact. You *sensed* him. He had star quality, animal magnetism, authority and presence, to everyone who met or knew him, in large ineluctable doses. If you analyzed his looks, feature by feature, particularly in the latter years, you came up with a droop-eyed, rumple-suited, beak-nosed little fellow. The secret of *his* impact was yours. If you warranted his total attention, his eyes and voice alone made him irresistible. When he wanted something.

He always wanted something. The best of everything. *Christina* was, and remains, a shining example of Ari's tasteful wants. There are, have been, and will be bigger yachts, more beautiful yachts, faster yachts, and more expensive yachts. But when *Christina* was launched in 1954, she immediately became the ultimate status symbol yacht to the haves and the have-nots alike.

Canny Mr. Onassis knew how to spend money, when to spend it, and when not to. With *Christina*, he ricocheted from one end of the pole to the other. He bought a war surplus Canadian frigate in 1952 from John Shapiro, who was then a Baltimore scrap dealer. Shapiro owned a number of vessels which he planned to break up for scrap. Somehow, he sold one of them, the *Stormont*, to Onassis for $35,000 and he has been sorry about it ever since . . . but not very, since he does not even pretend to be a yachtsman. Besides, the *Stormont* was only one of ten obsolete ships that Onassis bought at the time, and Shapiro had no idea that Onassis intended to convert the *Stormont* into a yacht, nor did he care. Onassis sent his war surplus vessels to Germany to be converted into whalers. All but one. *Christina*, the most beautiful of sea butterflies, came out of her cocoon a year and a half and a million and a half dollars later. When she left the shipyard in Kiel, the meticulous Germans who had converted her were, and still are, in awe of her perfections. *Christina* was luxury supreme, the best of everything that money could buy, and Onassis meant her to be just that.

There was one jarring note, reported in the press no less than a thousand times by whoever was writing or talking about *the* yacht. The Greeks are a funny bunch when it comes to taste. Onassis certainly had taste and style in the jewels and cars and women and yachts that he bought, but in bar stools, his taste was downright vulgar. The bar stools on board *Christina* were covered with a very personal part of a whale's anatomy for your fanny to sit on, and had whale's teeth for your feet to rest on. Ugh. If you asked for a double drink and rested your eyes on the portrait of young Christina above the blue lapis-lazuli fireplace, your mind was still where your behind was perched. It has also been reported that Stavros Niarchos covers the bar stools on his huge new *Atlantis* with the same, shall we say, fabric. Maybe the Greeks have a word for it, but the word could very well be "barbaric." If those bar stools were intended as conversation pieces, it makes you wonder what in the world these people talk about.

§

Christina has many redeeming, indeed famous-first, features for a yacht. One of the first accoutrements Onassis ordered was a canary-yellow amphibian airplane to be carried on her upper deck, and you don't see one of those on just any old yacht. With binoculars handy to identify the bigger and better boats as they slip past, that canary-yellow flash up top assured you that you were looking at the real *Christina*.

Resting forward, not far below the amphibian's deck space, are the Onassis private quarters, seen only by close friends. The private quarters consist of a sitting room, a bedroom, and a bath. The bathroom more than makes up for those whale foreskins in the bar. It seems silly to say that the most famous room on the entire yacht is the master bathroom, but it's a killer. It's a symphony in Siena marble, copied faithfully from the bath of King Minos of ancient Crete. Very few people, even kings, bathed in those days, so thank heaven the Cretan king was the Mr. Clean of his day and built himself such a gorgeous bathroom for Onassis to copy. The master bath on *Christina* is not only the number-one tourist attraction among guests, but its tub has been the site of some pretty racy and exclusive parties. The Greeks are a wild, party-loving bunch, and Onassis was never known as a shy flower.

Onassis had a serious social side, exemplified by his deep and everlasting friendship with Sir Winston Churchill. As is the case with most *hommes fatales*, Onassis was a man's man far more than he was ever a ladies' man. Women were necessary—he collected them carefully and nurtured them well—but men were vital to him. Obviously, Sir Winston wasn't one for the marble bath tub scene, but he did get stuck in the mosaic swimming pool once, and all hell broke loose when it happened.

The oval pool on *Christina* is equipped with a hydraulic lift that converts the bottom of the pool into a dance floor with the flick of a push button. Churchill and Onassis had a favorite game. Onassis would place two chairs in the center of the empty mosaic oval and he and Sir Winston would sit in the waterless pool riding up and down, the way kids do in elevators.

One afternoon, the mosaic oval got stuck near the bottom level. A wild scene ensued, with Onassis screaming at the engineer to fix the motor and fix it fast. Onassis climbed out, threatening nothing less than off-with-your-head for the poor engineer; Sir Winston was nevertheless aristocratically stranded in his chair, unable to get out of the pool. Churchill quietly suggested that a screwdriver might do more to solve the problem than would his host's suggestions as to what the engineer could do, where he could go, and what his future might be. Onassis cooled off, and as per Sir Winston's suggestion, the engineer came forth with a screwdriver. Moments later the dance floor-swimming pool bottom rose majestically to the top, delivering its valuable cargo safely. Churchill was eighty-five at the time, hardly the age to be scrambling out of swimming pools, but certainly knowledgeable about screwdrivers.

Churchill impressed Onassis more than did any other man, and the tenderness of Ari's feeling toward him was apparent to all who saw them together. Sir Winston and his darling Clementine were honored guests aboard *Christina* at least once each summer and winter, in the Mediterranean and the Caribbean. Onassis directed himself to Sir Winston almost to the exclusion of any other guest. At the end of one long Caribbean cruise he gave Sir Winston a gold cigar box for his birthday. The box had a map of each of the islands they visited etched into the gold: St. Lucia, Tobago, and Puerto Rico were engraved on one side; Antigua, Martinique, and Trinidad on the other. Written in the center was, "Happy Birthday from Ari, November 30, 1960." It was one of Churchill's favorite possessions, and one of countless presents that Onassis gave him.

When Onassis' tempestuous romance with Maria Callas began, it strained his most valuable friendship, since Lady Churchill was very fond of Tina Onassis. Lady Churchill was cool toward Callas during the diva's ten-year affair with Onassis. Like the Churchills, Tina was a part of Onassis' conservative side. She loved sailing a small Star class boat, and those who knew her well said that she was never happier than when she was sailing alone in her little Star. She may have been happy when the all-important Churchills were with them, but she was often desolate aboard *Christina*, and apparently she had no strong desire to be the hostess with the mostest, nor did she play her part particularly well. She was remote and vague and unenthusiastic, even with close friends, and took no pleasure from the luxe, the infinite privileges, or the fabulous guests who came to her husband's favorite home. In Tina's defense, the yacht belonged only to Onassis and he wanted neither advice nor aid when it came to running it. He planned everything with no help from his wife or any of his other women. He dominated *Christina* completely. She was a one-man yacht and they shared the same heartbeat.

In the years before the breakup of Onassis' marriage to Tina, before his romance with Callas, before the intensifying of his carefully structured feud with Stavros Niarchos, and long, long before his second wife, Jacqueline Kennedy, became part of his story, *Christina* and Ari shared whatever sybaritic pleasures they chose, singing their own sybaritic songs. These were the best years of their lives. Every king, every queen, and every famous or infamous person in the world of international society was invited and came to see and be entertained by Ari and his yachting lady, *Christina*. The qualifications for an invitation were simple. Be rich or famous, powerful or beautiful, and you were sure to be invited. If you happened to be all four you were a shoo-in, and there were numerous qualifiers in that position, happily. Nothing made Onassis happier than someone who was someone.

When Prince Rainier married Princess Grace, Onassis wouldn't have missed it for the world. Mrs. Bob Considine and Art Buchwald, two famous columnists and chums, were scooped up by Onassis one day and taken aboard *Christina*. A lively chronicler of social scenes all over the world, Millie Considine describes *that* scene thus:

"We had just arrived for the wedding week, and it was early morning when we ran into Ari in the bar at the Hôtel de Paris. He invited us to lunch on *Christina*, and the moment we got aboard we went over to the deck on the port side and watched as Prince Rainier steamed out on his tiny yacht, *Deo Juvante*, to fetch his bride-to-be off the *S.S. Constitution*. Since we were the only guests aboard, and it would be some time before Rainier came back with his future princess, Ari took the time to give us a tour of *Christina*. He loved showing her off. The suites were fantastically large and the paintings were all priceless. The bar was really king-sized, and the bar interested Art Buchwald and me the most, not just for the drinking. Ari told us that the bar stools, which looked as if they were covered with drum heads, were actually covered with the foreskin of a whale's penis. That alone gave Buchwald and me fodder for conversation for some time to come, especially Buchwald.

"A few nights later, Art was seated at a dinner party

next to Betsy Drake, who was married to Cary Grant at the time and seemed like a prim, proper, and remote girl. Thinking it would shock Betsy out of her cool, Art told her about the bar stools covered with the foreskin of a whale's penis. Betsy looked nonplussed for a moment, and then she exclaimed, 'Oh, Moby's Dick!' *That* broke some ice.

"But back to that first day. We all had caviar and some ouzo, the milky licorice-tasting Greek drink that Ari favored. When Rainier sailed back from the *Constitution* with Grace, who was wearing a ridiculous big white organdy hat that she had to clutch constantly to keep it from blowing away, we leaned over the side of *Christina* and looked down, and believe me, from the *Christina* we had to look *way* down at *Deo Juvante*. The entire harbor was bedlam, with cannons booming, planes and helicopters circling and fluttering around, and fireworks exploding overhead throwing out thousands of small Monegasque flags. We bombarded the happy pair from *Christina* with pink and white carnations shot out of special small cannons, floating down in little parachutes. The Prince was beaming and waving. Grace was hanging onto her hat for dear life. It was *quite* a day.

"During that week of festivities preceding the Royal wedding, we all ended up every night at a nightclub in the Casino where we joined Ari. We drank more champagne than I ever knew existed. At about four A.M., when the Casino closed, Ari would walk across the plaza like a Pied Piper, with the orchestra and those of us who had lasted still following along with him, all singing at the top of our lungs. We'd stop at the Café de Paris for breakfast and dance on the sidewalk while the orchestra played for us and everyone who cared to join us. Then he would take us back aboard *Christina* — music, strangers, and all — and we would dance and play until dawn. It was fiesta time, and as far as most of us were concerned Onassis was top banana, not Rainier."

§

In 1962, nearly ten years after the *Stormont* had become the *Christina*, Onassis bought Skorpios, an island in the Ionian Sea near Corfu. That's the right side of the tracks for a Greek island; the Aegean Sea, where most of the rich Greeks' private islands lie, is hotter and windier than the Ionian Sea and nowhere near as nice. Skorpios, named for its scorpion shape, is larger than all of Monaco by a hundred acres, a fact that always delighted Onassis. Unlike Monte Carlo, Skorpios is off limits to the common man, who cannot get within a cannon shot of it uninvited, so there is no problem about privacy or over-crowding. After so many years of wandering, Onassis and his yacht found a home base of their own, and a Greek one at that. Onassis owned innumerable homes, among them his villa in Glyfada near Athens, and an apartment on the Avenue Foch in Paris, and he kept permanent hotel suites at Claridge's in London and at the Pierre Hotel in New York, but Skorpios signaled his return to Greece and gave *Christina* a jetty of her own, at least, to drop anchor near. (No bay at Skorpios was deep enough to harbor her.) Onassis, the Turkish-born Greek, was at home in his native land at last.

Regardless of the beauty and privacy of Skorpios, Monte Carlo was always the real glamour base for Ari and *Christina*. When you arrived from the Nice airport and wound down into Monte Carlo by car, not to see *Christina* gleaming creamily in the port was certain indication that you had arrived off season. For years, the parties on *Christina* were, to put it mildly, sensational. The mosaic swimming pool not only doubled as a dance floor; on party nights it could be transformed into a Roman fountain with colored jets of water tinkling softly, but never drowning out the music. Onassis was music mad. For big parties on *Christina*, he would have flown in a French orchestra, some of his beloved bouzouki players from Athens, a favorite trio from Mexico to sing romantic songs, and some flamencos from Madrid to while the night away. He had flown in everything but the Rochester Fife and Drum Corps. To continue to do so, it became "necessary" for him to buy Olympic Airways.

The personal whims of the really rich are mind-boggling to normal human beings. Now that he had an airline, there was not much more that even an Onassis could desire. He had wine, women, song, a wife, children, money, power, and at least four shirts. He may *not* have had a good tailor. Rich or no, Onassis was one of the world's worst dressed men. He was certainly the most unpressed. He cared nothing for clothes, and the few he really liked were old. But he would spend $20,000 or more on a party without turning a hair, and drop another five thousand on top of it for tips and extras.

His favorite French bread was flown to the yacht daily from Paris. To do so cost about $200 a day but, "Let 'em eat bread," he might say, and he was paying for it. A certain type of Greek orange that he loved was flown weekly from Glyfada to wherever the yacht was. On one trip, when Garbo was aboard, he secretly planned a private film festival to please her, getting hold of all of her films as a surprise. Garbo wept as they were shown. She had not seen any of them for many years. She wept for her own lost beauty and for so many of her friends from the great film days who were now dead, and Ari wept with her, loving the whole scene he had provided.

When Jacqueline Kennedy married Aristotle Onassis in 1968, he met his match in Big Spenders. They were married on Skorpios and they honeymooned on *Christina*, with her children, not his, going along for the ride. In the first year of their marriage, Onassis dribbled $2 million dollars' worth of jewels Jackie's way in multiple-carat doses. Jackie came closer to shaking up *Christina* than any other woman.

After all, she was used to the best in everything, from creature comforts to service. Twelve sets of pale pink sheets, monogrammed by nuns in an Italian convent, were used by Madame Onassis wherever she went. Whenever she got out of bed, discarding her pale pink nightgown on the floor, whoosh, fresh pink sheets were automatically put on.

The first Christmas of their marriage was spent cruising on *Christina* with Caroline and John Kennedy. The Onassis children and the Kennedy children never particularly cottoned to one another, partially because of the difference in their ages. With his marriage to the widow

Kennedy, Ari Onassis began an ambivalent life, dividing his non-business time between his wife and stepchildren, both of whom were extremely fond of him, and his own son and daughter. Rarely the twain would meet, and even more rarely aboard *Christina*. Ari remained faithful to the yacht, however, and continued to spend as much time aboard as ever. Jackie was a sensation everywhere they went, as is her norm, and Ari loved it. Photographers dogged their heels, snapping pictures from behind every bush and tree. But he missed *Christina*'s and his world, when the two of them had been the stars.

§

Gradually, the character of both the man and the yacht changed. *Christina* still belonged to Ari and no one but Ari, but the years began to tell on him. The scene was old now, too, and there were few new or fresh faces that even began to live up to the glamour and excitement of days gone by. Ari had met and conquered them all. Churchill was dead, Garbo was reclusive. Eugenie Niarchos, Tina's sister, was dead. Tina had married Niarchos, her dead sister's widower, causing a new rift of titanic proportions between the two men, as if the old feud were not enough. And then Tina, too, was dead. Princess Grace and Callas had nothing to do with Jackie, nor she with them. Onassis continued to see Callas whenever he chose, but then again Jackie, not Callas, was Mrs. Aristotle Socrates Onassis — the title Callas had never achieved.

When Alexander Onassis, Ari's only son, was killed in an airplane crash in Athens in January 1973, his death was a bell that tolled for Onassis himself. Aristotle Onassis was never the same after the death of Alexander. He was devastated by the loss of his son. He was tired of it all and he returned to *Christina* time and time again to bind up his wounds as best he could. He was getting old quickly, he was no longer well at all, and nothing excited him anymore. The parties were few and far between, and the old Pied Piper danced no more in the streets of Monte Carlo.

When Stavros Niarchos brought his huge new *At-*

lantis into Monte Carlo, everyone expected the towering, raging competitive angers of the old days to repeat themselves. But instead, Ari paid a polite visit and soon after that the word spread around that the feud was over. Ari actually didn't give a hoot about the big new Niarchos yacht. The two men apparently declared temporary peace with each other. There was nothing left for Onassis to compete for. He had it all made, and the brass rings had all been caught.

"All that really counts these days is money," he said once, long ago. He was right, at least by his own rules. When he died in Paris in the American Hospital at the age of sixty-nine, he left an estate valued at somewhere between five hundred million and one billion dollars. That kind of money does count. His last will made his only child, Christina, a billionairess. Jackie was provided for reasonably well. Caroline and John Kennedy were the recipients of million-dollar trust funds, and Onassis' three sisters were left lavishly well off. Christina Onassis wasted no time taking control of Ari's empire, as was his desire. Maybe he was right about money. No one seemed to care very much when he died, or that he died, except his daughter. All that seemed to matter to anyone about Onassis was how much money he had, and who got what in the end.

In two years' time, Christina Onassis had lost her brother, her mother, and her father. She was at her father's bedside in the American hospital in Paris at the end. Jackie was in New York; she flew immediately to Paris with Senator Edward Kennedy, where they joined Christina and a few close relatives for the chartered flight to Actium, the nearest airport to Skorpios, carrying Onassis' body on the plane with them. Mrs. Hugh Auchincloss, Jackie's mother, and Caroline and John Kennedy joined the family group there and they were driven by limousine to Nidri, the coast opposite Skorpios, where *Christina* waited. On the way to Nidri, John-John Kennedy put his fingers in his ears and stuck his tongue out at the Greeks lining the road. Christina changed cars, immediately starting rumors of a rift between the two women. The sad party boarded *Christina* and embarked on the short voyage home for Onassis, his last voyage on the yacht that he loved. He was buried in a cypress grove alongside Alexander, who had been dead only two years, almost to the day.

All the obituaries dwelt on money, money, money, and how Christina Onassis would handle it. The gossip columns tore Jackie apart for not having been with him when he died, but the world cared little, if at all, that he was gone.

If yachts could care, his beautiful *Christina* cared. He left her nothing, but she had been the best-kept lady in yachting, and his love for her was genuine. She will never be the same again without Onassis, roaming the seas of the yachting world, masterless and alone.

6
Stavros' Great White Whale of a Yacht

When Stavros Niarchos brought *Atlantis,* the newest and largest of all the many yachts he has owned, into the harbor at Monte Carlo in the summer of 1974, he ended one era of yachting and began a new one. Stavros Niarchos can confuse you without turning a hair. That's yachting for you, too. Just when you get used to one lifestyle, someone blows the whistle and starts another one. Niarchos blew the whistle loud and clear with his super, super yacht *Atlantis.*

Big yachts were supposed to be a thing of the past, and if you still had one you were either stuck with it from the old days or you were old-fashioned and liked it that way. Oh, some lovely people, without apology, still clung to the beautiful motor yachts that were built in the rich years before World War II, and there were the exceptions like *La Belle Simone* and *Carinthia VI*. But they, like *Atlantis*, were the exceptions.

The rule, in the decades of the Sixties and Seventies, was that every really with-it newly commissioned yacht was 100 feet or less. The smart boys and the smart money would have nothing to do with any Leviathan-like yachts. Gianni Agnelli, Fiat's mastermind and pacesetter, never had a big yacht. Instead, he owns some of the fastest and most exciting boats that the Med or any other sea has ever borne, all of them less than 100 feet long. The Aga Khan took up the trend toward the shorter yacht and built *Kalamoun*, a speedy 98-foot beauty, when, had he wanted to, he could have built a 998-foot yacht. He, too, was interested in speed and maneuverability, and *Kalamoun* does a phenomenal 50 knots. She was christened in 1973 and was an old hand, well shaken down and used to her fast-paced life, by the summer of 1974.

Enter *Atlantis* and Niarchos.

Atlantis is the biggest private yacht afloat in the world today. She is 380 feet long and almost 900 tons heavier than *Christina*. *Atlantis* is longer than either Babe Ruth's or Hank Aaron's average home run, and the water she displaces would fill to overflowing more than one million magnums of champagne. She cost Niarchos only about $8.5 million. See how lucky you can be? Especially if you are Greek and own shipyards.

Why Stavros Niarchos decided to build the largest private yacht afloat is an enigma. Was it to take the title away from his old rival, Aristotle Onassis? Was it to give his wife Tina a larger yacht than she had had as plain Mrs. Onassis? You can find perfectly valid reasons for almost anything the Greeks do. At least Greeks can. But what in the world Niarchos wanted with *Atlantis* is still a big question mark, no matter what anyone tells you.

Niarchos already owned *Creole*, the most heart-catchingly beautiful three-masted black schooner ever built. Wherever she went, yachtsmen felt a stirring to possess her. Even a landlubber would have robbed a bank to own her. Her beauty affected one and all who saw her. She now lies unused in Piraeus, with a skeleton crew and a rotting hull. Anyone who wants her can have her for about a million dollars, but it would take another million to repair, refit, and refurbish her. Poor beautiful *Creole*. Niarchos also had *Mercury*, the forerunner of the short, fast yachts. The 102-foot *Mercury* was the first gas-turbine yacht capable of doing over 50 knots. Between *Creole* and *Mercury*, he had everything that yachting could offer. Why *Atlantis*?

Maybe the man who had everything had to have everything more. The supposed—and cleverly contrived—feud between Niarchos and Onassis probably gave birth to *Atlantis*, though Niarchos' twenty-two-year-old son, Phillipe, insists that no feud existed. "My father simply decided to build a new boat," he says. "And naturally, he wanted the best that money could buy. Quality was his aim, not quantity. After all, there are many bigger ships in my father's fleet." Niarchos said nothing. That's the best way of saying anything.

§

Atlantis is the best of some things and the worst of others, but one special accessory sets her apart from all other yachts. It is a dark gray box, about the size of an average television set, that sits unobtrusively on the bridge. It houses an ITT Satellite Navigator, one of only two in the world carried by a passenger ship. The other one is on Cunard Line's *Queen Elizabeth II*. The Navigator can be programmed for any voyage, for its computer is in constant contact with an orbiting ITT satellite. Let's say you decide to cruise from Istanbul to Venice. Each time *Atlantis* moves sixty feet through the water, her progress is noted by the satellite, which beams back a precise position fix and steering directions. These appear in luminous digits on the Navigator's face, and the helmsman corrects his course according to the computer's orders. "We could hook the Navigator directly into the ship's steering mechanism," says Captain Tsioros, a veteran Niarchos cargo ship skipper, whose first captaincy aboard a private yacht is on *Atlantis*. "But then I wouldn't have anything to do."

Another surprise offered by *Atlantis* is that although Niarchos is a billionaire, he is a prudent one, in his own imprudent way. *Atlantis* operates with a basic crew of seventeen, which is one man for every twenty-two feet of yacht. Never before has such a large yacht been able to operate perfectly, or operate at all, with that few in crew. The key to this marvel is near-total automation, which takes care of operational difficulties and the high cost of help at the same time. The number of crew on the housekeeping staff varies, depending on the number of guests occupying the twelve guest suites. Phillipe Niarchos quite unselfconsciously revealed the mode of living on *Atlantis* by saying, "When just my father and I are living aboard we make do with only two cooks and three stewards." Some servant crunch, eh? The poor darlings.

Aside from the Navigator, *Atlantis* is a boring boat, and ugly to boot. No one seems to find her beautiful, special, exciting, worth the money she cost, or enviable. Except Niarchos, and who's going to quarrel with him?

Atlantis is full of standard, old-fashioned features. Same old swimming pool, for instance, almost a replica of the one on *Christina*. (Did Niarchos copy Onassis? Would Macy's tell Gimbel's?) The mosaic bottom rises hydraulically to become a dance floor, just like *Christina*'s. In the midst of the blue oval, there is a design that combines a helm and a compass. There is a helicopter landing pad on the upper deck. A Rolls-Royce and a small Volkswagen Karmann Ghia that Niarchos prefers to drive are stowed below, both painted metallic blue. There are speedboats, water-skiing boats, and launches. There's a sauna and a gymnasium, and a cinema, of course, which seats forty. Normal, everyday yachting comforts. The olive-wood paneled library in the main salon has shelves full of who-done-its, but it's doubtful if any of them are as intriguing as the life of *Atlantis*' owner has been.

Atlantis was put together nicely, if traditionally, for the comfort of her guests. In each of the twelve guest suites — not rooms, mind you, but suites — you live with a painter. Here again, *Atlantis* resembles *Christina*. Niarchos' guest suites are named for painters: Onassis' for

Greek islands. As for the paintings themselves, Niarchos and Onassis must have shopped in the same auction rooms and galleries. In their world, expensive is expensive, and the more expensive the better. In the *Atlantis'* suites, Klee, Dali, Van Velde, or Poliakoff are there to keep you company with at least one (and, more often, two or three) of their paintings staring you in the eye. Little things, like matching sheets and towels in a different color for each suite, were specially made, keyed to the predominant color in the paintings. The Greek housekeeping staff is kept busy trying to figure out whether the blue towels and blue sheets belong to the Dali or the Klee quarters.

Remember Onassis' bar on the *Christina*? Niarchos' bar stools are covered with whale skin, too. *Atlantis'* bar has two huge Elvis Presleys, executed by none other than our own Andy Warhol, aiming mean guns at you. The Elvis pictures look ridiculous in that setting, and the bar is tasteless, uncomfortable, and cold. The only Greek touch on the whole huge yacht are some smashing Poucette murals in the main stairwell and hall. They are a riot of reds and blacks and oranges and yellows and were "influenced" by some ancient frescoes found on the Mediterranean island of Thera. Thera, according to several modern archeologists and Niarchos, could have been the site of the dreamlike lost continent of Atlantis. Whatever you say, Mr. Niarchos, sir.

The lavish comfort of *Atlantis* is most apparent in the sunken main salon. It's huge for a yacht, and big enough for a country home—that is, if you consider forty-five by thirty feet a fair-sized room. The salon is carpeted in something resembling four-inch-deep white velvet. The walls are panels of olive wood, and there's a working chrome fireplace that gave a bad turn to the insurance underwriters—but Niarchos won that round. After all, no self-respecting yacht is without a working fireplace. Everything that can be chrome *is* chrome, and that does away with another two or three unnecessary crew members who spend years of their time polishing brass on other yachts.

There's a fake Gauguin over the fireplace, but everyone who is anyone knows it's a good reproduction, and they know why. The salon is exposed to fresh sea air, while all of the guest suites and Niarchos' private quarters are sealed and air-conditioned. Frantic art experts begged Niarchos to leave the real Gauguin, which he owns, on dry land, which he did.

Niarchos' private quarters are Spartan. Strange how many powerful men, richer than Croesus, have cell-like private bedrooms. The only furniture is Niarchos' double bed, with a small lowboy beside it. Half a dozen priceless personal icons hang above the bed, and that is all. How's that for no frills?

§

Atlantis has a strange impact. She is more ship than yacht in appearance, whether you're on her or looking at her. She's too big. Seeing her at anchor in the harbor of Monte Carlo makes you feel that Niarchos is mad. Here's a huge, ugly, shiplike yacht that outweighs the *Nina*, the *Pinta*, and the *Santa Maria*, combined, by more than 2,000 tons. Sort of makes you want to discover America again. Why, when everyone is building small yachts, is this vast white whale the cynosure of all eyes? It must be money talking again.

John Bannenberg, an Australian-English interior designer of grand repute, moans when he mentions *Atlantis*. He had nothing to do with her, but he is one of the most avant-garde interior designers in yachting, and his opinion is respected. "*Atlantis* looks as if she were conceived and built in the Fifties," Bannenberg says. "When you *think* what Niarchos could have done! He had everything at his beck and call to work with. Shipyards, endless money, and the taste to choose from the finest of everything the yachting world has to offer. He has years of knowledge and experience in every phase of yachting. He built *Mercury*, a yacht years ahead of her time. How *could* he build *Atlantis*? It's not in character at all. *Atlantis* is neither fast, nor, beyond the Satellite Navigator, is she new in any sense of the word, and why does any private yacht really need that sort of equipment? It's all James Bond, and that's passé, too."

§

The one and only summer that Tina Livanos Onassis Blandford Niarchos spent aboard her husband's new mammoth white monster was one of relative restraint. In August they were in Sardinia, where they invited ninety chums aboard for a seated dinner. It was their first and only large party of the season. The Aga Khan's Week of the Straits was in full bloom. One hundred and sixty-seven yachts were racing, and more than 800 yachts were in Sardinia for the occasion. The island was entirely surrounded by boats, catamarans, schooners, ketches, dhows and scows, sloops, yawls, and what-have-you that floats. All the heavy personalities of yachting were present, accounted for, and wanting to be asked aboard *Atlantis.*

The ninety international darlings who were invited to dine had one thing in common. They were all Chiefs. There wasn't a nook or a cranny available for an Indian. Most of the guests were also owners of important yachts, and well aware of their social clout. Although that bunch occasionally hurl champagne glasses at each other—which always seems to make headlines—the evening was unmarked by any incident of world-shattering social impact.

Tina, as usual, let her husband run the show. Dinner was served at round tables on deck. It was a shame not to use the dining room. The room itself is instantly forgettable, but the two Degas, two Renoirs, and the Utrillo hanging on the walls are not. No amount of extravagant Georgian silver, no gourmet delights, and no glittering guests can compete with those paintings.

On the night of the party, the wind proceeded to blow, as it blows only in Sardinia—even more reason to use the dining room. Nine days out of thirteen the never-ending wind convinces you that if it were not for the Aga Khan, you would no more set foot in Sardinia than Napoleon would set up housekeeping on Elba if he whizzed through again. On *Atlantis*, canvas baffles are used for parties on deck to shield hair, flowers, food, thin-stemmed glasses, tempers, and sanity. It's hard to be civil, much less civilized, with that wind blowing, but at least you don't have to worry too much about conversation, as no one can hear you anyway what with the music, the wind, and other guests' primary preoccupation with themselves.

The guest list included the Aga Khan, the Loel Guinnesses, Lord Camrose, Lady Joan Aly Khan, a sprinkling of Rothschilds, Schlesingers, Bulgaris, Lord Snowdon and, thank God, the lighthearted David Niven. Everyone knew pretty much what they were going to talk about since they have nothing new to say to each other unless someone dies. The subject was *Atlantis*. Some oh'd, some ah'd. Others ugh'ed, but only later when they were safely ashore and out of Niarchos' earshot.

Criticism is the one thing a yacht owner can count on when he brings forth a new yacht. The yachting crowd is the most fault-finding group extant. If they like your sundeck, they hate your launches. If they love your bridge, they knock your chef — or steal him. Even a Niarchos is not immune to the bitchery, and especially not with a yacht like *Atlantis*.

§

Most of *Atlantis*'s first summer was spent running back and forth between Sardinia and Monte Carlo. She became a bigger tourist attraction in Monte Carlo than even Princess Grace, and when *Christina* pulled in, Onassis and his guests were promptly invited to inspect the new Niarchos baby. Ari came right over.

It was one of the last times the two men saw each other. Ari, naturally, was polite about *Atlantis*, but his tune changed when he got back aboard *Christina*. He was positively gleeful that Niarchos had seen fit to copy him so thoroughly. Ari and his guests agreed that *Atlantis* was nothing special and that the best of her style was a direct copy of *Christina*. Wood-burning fireplaces, painted murals, a swimming pool that became a dance floor, naming the staterooms—it was all duplication. (Conspicuous by her absence was Jackie, who had declined the invitation to visit *Atlantis*.)

In October of that year, Tina Niarchos died in Paris. Her death left the largest private yacht in the world without a mistress. For the moment.

One thing is for sure. Stavros Niarchos claims to be as fond of *Atlantis* as Onassis was of *Christina*. No island burial for him. He plans to be buried on *Atlantis*. Not from her. On her. When he goes, she goes. He has written a provision into his will that, upon his death, she is to be sent to the bottom with his body, where the two of them will presumably join the mysterious lost continent for which the yacht was named.

7
A Date With Nefertiti

If you have a loose $60,000 just lying around and you don't know what to do with yourself next summer, why don't you charter a yacht for a week? *Nefertiti* might be available. If she is, snap her up. *Nefertiti* is newish. And biggish. And gorgeous. And only $60,000 a week, give or take a little. Mostly give. Not every yacht costs that much to charter, thank Neptune, but *Nefertiti* is a special case. She is probably the biggest, best, and most luxuriously expensive yacht available in these sensuous Seventies. Besides, if you asked Christina Onassis or Niarchos or Levitt or Revson (when he was alive) to charter *Christina* or *Atlantis* or *La Belle Simone* or *Ultima II* for a tiny week or so, the answer would be no. They never rent out their boats. Nor does the Queen of England.

    Nefertiti is 202 feet long and she was built in Bilbao, Spain, in 1973. Her owner is the Trondheim Shipping

Company, and whoever *they* are, they do not give out their names to any of us common folk. They are a syndicate, and syndicates love anonymity. David Halsey-Marine, a charter firm in London, can arrange for *Nefertiti* to be at you beck and call, once your Dun & Bradstreet has been checked out favorably. She does have the prettiest swimming pool of the aforementioned lot, and she's a lovely yacht, although her interior trappings give designers Raymond Loewy and John Bannenberg a bad case of the shudders. *Nefertiti* is sort of an expensive Holiday Inn of the high seas. She was built to be chartered, rather than to be a one-man dream boat. This is not to say that her real owners don't enjoy her. They do, but chartering helps to defray some (and only some) of her costs. She is rated *100A1 in Lloyd's Register, and at sixty grand a week, she certainly should be. Her captain is German, with a properly snooty British accent, and she carries a crew of fourteen to sixteen, all dying to serve you.

Nefertiti has no problems, though her paying guests have been known to have theirs. A summer or so ago she was chartered out for two cruises that got mixed reviews, from crew and guests alike. First, she was chartered to an Arab with a mania for gambling. He directed the captain to hug the southern coast of France so that three white Cadillacs from his stable of cars could trail along beside her on the winding cliff roads between St. Tropez and Monte Carlo. You see, the captain had to be ready to put into port posthaste whenever a gambling fit hit the Saudi sugar daddy. The Cads were there to rush him to the nearest casino so he could blow a bundle of that lovely oil money. The crew could never bring themselves to speak fondly of the Arab group during or after that charter, and the chef got downright testy about all the lamb and rice that was being served from the floor of the main salon daily and nightly—and forklessly—while facing Mecca. Lamb and rice, lamb and rice—for the full two weeks of the Arab charter, and nary a crêpe suzette.

§

The next summer charterer was Bud Seretean. He's the majority stockholder in RCA, so the best things in his life don't have to be free. Bud and his warm, pretty wife, Farol, live in Chattanooga, Tennessee, although, as one of their closest friends rhapsodized, "*Money* is their home." Well, money is a great place to live, and money certainly made it possible for the Sereteans to charter *Nefertiti* — and not just for one stingy single week but for a full, glorious two. They invited nine friends to come traveling and to break bread upon the waters with them. Some pretty hair-raising tales resulted, as all nine guests were strong and independent characters as well as friends. They had never been to sea together, and none of them had *ever* spent any time on a big yacht before.

Farol Seretean has a habit of flinging unlikely people together. She stands back and smiles and bows when it all works out, but when explosive temperaments drive guests to each other's throats, Farol has been known to vaporize. Mixing odd types is her preference, and it assures her that there will be none of those dull dinner parties with the same old compatible people playing bridge, making polite conversation, and boring themselves and each other right into oblivion. Not for Farol. Bud Seretean planned the trip and Farol planned the people. She had a great aider and abetter in the person of Jim Nabors, who plays games on television as well as everywhere else, and this sure-fire gamble with disaster or glory appealed to both of them. The guest list also included two extra women, one of whom was separated from her husband, although she didn't know it at the time. The rest of the bunch did, however.

When the plans for the Seretean-*Nefertiti* cruise were complete, the group assembled in Nice. They were transported from there to San Remo in Italy — for reasons explained later by Bud Seretean — where they boarded *Nefertiti*. The happy ship of fools embarked for a well-planned cruise that was to take some unplanned turns.

Bud Seretean had sent out letters of invitation to his guests in May. His first letter was in memo form, with guests' names listed alphabetically from the top. The memo was headed, "First Annual Seretean Vacation Extravaganza." And it read:

"Welcome to the club!

"Here is a rough outline of what is in store for you.

"We will board the yacht *Nefertiti* in either Antibes or San Remo for a fifteen-day cruise in the Mediterranean, primarily in French and Spanish waters, commencing Sunday, August 4th. Disembarkation will be in Antibes on Monday morning, August 19th. The Nice airport services Antibes.

"In order to assist the captain and chef, we will need the following information from each of you:

1. Your nationality and passport number.

2. Any special dietary requirements, or any foods you particularly dislike.

3. Your alcohol, soft drink, mix and other beverage preferences and brands.

4. Brand of cigarettes, if you smoke.

5. Please indicate any special interests, such as swimming, snorkeling, sightseeing, entertainment ashore."

"In future bulletins I will provide you with specifics about the following:

1. Our yacht.

2. Our itinerary.

3. Our guests.

4. Wardrobe requirements."

That was enough for the moment. The invitees stood back, thought it over, accepted, and promptly went out to Saks, Gucci, their dentists, doctors, astrologists, and analysts. Then they waited with bated breath for the next bulletin. None of them committed themselves to anything beyond their arrival time in Nice. No one came up with any food or booze preferences. They sent their passport numbers, and that was about it.

The second bulletin went out toward the end of May. In it, Bud Seretean's secretary really spelled it out. The bulletin gave the length of the yacht, the accommodations available, plus other glorious details, and threw in the line, "You will be the Sereteans' guests for the entire cruise, from the time you get to the airport in Nice until you return to Nice for your flight home." Airplane reservations had been made for everyone and the group would travel together on an Air France flight that left New York in the evening and arrived in Nice the following morning. She also rapped all the recalcitrants on the knuckles for not having come up with information requested, especially what they wanted to eat.

A third bulletin, at the end of June, informed guests that since there were no stated preferences, special emphasis would be made on fresh fruits and juices, diet soft drinks, assorted low-calorie cheeses, and vegetable and fruit salads. The memo also included the proposed itinerary, plus masses of descriptive information about the yacht, and a deck plan. The very last bulletin came from Bud Seretean in mid-July, telling the group that he would be in Nice a day early to make sure that all was shipshape, and that he would look forward to meeting them at the airport in Nice. Everything was working nicely. So far. But let Bud Seretean tell you the rest.

"I flew over with Henry Lewis, one of my guests, the day before. I wanted to make sure that everything was all right. First of all, when we went aboard we had a talk with the chef. A number of my friends were diet-conscious, and I wanted to explain this to the chef. Now Henry and I have about a hundred words of French between us, I think. We tried to explain to him about no butter, no frying, skim milk, no calories, and all that. You should have seen his face. The poor guy. On top of it all, we arrived just after the Arab charter, which I knew nothing about at the time. The chef was having a hard enough time understanding what we were saying, and now we were trying to tell him that he was not supposed to do the only thing he knows how to do well. I had a hunch from the start that the whole arrangement with the chef was going to be a problem. He'd had a tough enough time with the Arabs.

"After that, Henry and I checked up and found out that there were no diet drinks aboard. I had ordered cases of them, but there was no such concoction in the south of France or in all of France, for that matter. The agent who orders the supplies told me we could get them out of London, so I said, 'Okay, *get* them out of London, I don't care where they come from, just *get* them.' I got a bill for about five hundred bucks six months later and I paid it, though we never got any diet drinks — out of London or anywhere else. None of us really cared that much. It's just that no matter how smooth it all looks, there are a thousand little things that can go wrong.

"I chartered a bus to meet Farol and the others at the Nice airport — our friends travel with a lot of luggage. By then, I had discovered that if we went out of a French port there was some rinky-dink rule that we had to pay extra in port taxes — you know how the French are — and it would save close to ten thousand dollars if we left from Italy. Okay, so we board the yacht in San Remo. And do you know what was going on in San Remo that day? They were having a big celebration. A speedboat race. They only have it once a year, and this year it happened to be racing around *my* yacht. No permissions or questions had been asked, of course. We couldn't get out of San Remo until the race was over because *Nefertiti* was what they were racing around. We finally got out, but not until late in the evening. It was fun, sure, but threw the whole schedule right off the bat.

"Next, and as I predicted, the chef was miserable. First of all, he had no way to produce what we wanted anyway. No French chef knows anything about diet foods and what he did provide was awful. I finally decided what had to be done, so I called him in and said, 'Okay, we have decided not to diet.' You should have seen his face then — he understood all right. Back he rushed to his *mille feuilles* and rich sauces. Our whole health food plan was finished, but at least the chef was happy for awhile."

Farol Seretean broke in. "The funniest thing that happened on the whole trip was all my fault. When we found out that we could not have diet food, I began by planning menus with the chef every day. Then I thought it might be fun if everyone took turns planning dinner for one evening. When it got to be Zetta Castle's turn, she was determined to do the best dinner of all, naturally. In the morning, she sent the chef ashore to get brussels sprouts.

He couldn't find brussels sprouts anywhere, and after what he had been through with us already, he didn't want to say so. When he got back to the yacht he was, well, he wasn't sober, though we didn't know it at the time.

"When we all met for cocktails at eight-thirty, Madame Castle had made such a fabulous menu that she wasn't going to let us spoil our appetites with anything silly like hors d'oeuvres. Jani, the steward, was serving drinks, but nothing else. Not even dinner, as it turned out. We sat there waiting and waiting, and getting hungry. At nine-thirty, I gave Zetta the evil eye and we marched out to the galley. There was the chef, drunk as a goat and sliding about in chesse souffle. 'A terrible thing has happened, Madame, I have dropped a souffle,' he said, as if we hadn't noticed. 'There will be a slight delay, Madame,' he said. 'Slight' isn't the word for it. He actually made another souffle, and this time we even heard it when—wouldn't you know—he dropped that one too.

"By now, it was eleven o'clock, and all tempers were frayed. Zetta and I got Jani, the steward, and said 'Just do *something*,' so he rallied around, the candles were lit on the table, we all sat down, and in came Jani and the waiter with some great silver trays. Can you guess what was on those trays? Seven courses of bread: brown bread, white bread, blue bread, black bread, and that was all. They presented that bread to us as if it was gold, and at that point, it was. We were all so hungry that we ate it as if it was Zetta's best gourmet dinner."

§

The Sereteans and guests had stopped in Monte Carlo, then gone on to St. Tropez. Bud takes up the story. "Monte Carlo was fine but none of us liked St. Tropez much. It's too small, and too crowded now. We were on our way to Spain and I asked the captain if there were any French islands we could see en route. He must have been used to catering to the antics of yachting groups, because he told me there was a nudist island and pointed it out on the chart. I said, 'You just stop there by accident, as if it wasn't

my idea, and I'll say, "Gee, I didn't know this was here." '
The captain cautioned me, however, that if you put a
tender down to go ashore, you have to disrobe. So I knew
all that, and we stopped at a small beach to swim and then
when one of the crew just accidentally pointed out the
nudist island, we all rushed back aboard the yacht and
grabbed the binoculars. My wife was beating me over the
head for my binoculars. But Nabors was the natural for this
one, and I really planned it with him in mind."

Jim Nabors lived up to expectations. He went bash-
ing ashore, naked as a jaybird. "I was better off with no
clothes on anyhow. When I was invited on the *Nefertiti*
trip, I had pasha-like visions of loafing around in luxury for
two weeks pretending I was the Shah of Iran, but no
chance. Farol put me in a closet. My single stateroom,
since I was the only single man, was smaller than I am. I
lived in that closet for the whole two weeks. One bunk. If
you closed the door you couldn't get out, if you opened it
you couldn't get in. Everyone else was in gorgeous suites
and I was in a room two feet wide with a bunk in it—so I
was *ready* to break out a little. Anyhow, I took off all my
clothes and went to the island. I walked around for about
an hour, feeling insecure, but I was completely ignored and
just getting comfortable when another guy, totally nude
and ugly, came up to me and said, 'Aren't you Gomer
Pyle?' Quick as a flash, I covered my private parts and said
'No!' and fled back to the yacht.

"The places we went to were a dream, and the best
of all was Formentor in Majorca. We came cruising into
that beautiful little jewel of a bay and went ashore to an almost unbelievably beautiful beach and a fantastic hotel.
None of us had ever even heard of Formentor before and
we all loved it. I loved Sardinia too, but that was later in
the trip, and from there on I could see personalities starting
to break down. I don't know why it is that if you put a
group of really good friends together, all successful and
fairly intelligent people, their natures change completely
on a yacht. Not always for the worse; they simply are not
the same people you knew ashore. Some of us came out intact, but some didn't."

Kay Starr and her husband, Woodie Gunther, were part of the cruise. Kay has been a popular singer and recording artist for so long that she was probably born in a trunk. But she hadn't anticipated that the trip would include those small headaches that can blow out of all proportion, even among the best of friends on the best of cruises. "When the Sereteans invited us on the *Nefertiti* trip," she said, "I really looked forward to it. I wanted to go on a big motor yacht, and knowing we would be in super luxury, I went out and bought this outfit and that outfit, and about fifty pairs of shoes to match everything. Naturally, the airline lost a bag for me, the one that had *all* my shoes in it, and all my makeup and eyelashes. I buy eyelashes by the ton, and I can do without shoes, but not those special eyelashes. I went out and bought some French eyelashes and makeup and about eight hundred dollars worth of shoes. My bag turned up five minutes before the trip was over, naturally. I planned to return the shoes to the stores when I got back. Coming back through customs, the guy who got lucky and drew me wanted me to pay duty on the shoes from California and the shoes from France as well. We had the slip, thank heavens, saying that my bag had been lost, but I am still up to my ears in shoes. Oh, the mix-ups.

"Hair was a big problem. None of the gals remembered about European electric current, and there was only one converter for Carmen curlers aboard, so we were all after it every night. Farol had the converter and she hid it from us. Boy, did we scream at her about that. On top of it all, I had a pair of Majorcan pearl earrings, and Farol had some that looked just like them, only hers cost whatever the moon would cost. She left them in an ashtray one night, and I thought they were mine. When hers turned up missing, we tore the yacht apart looking for them. Then I got home and found her earrings in my jewelry box, and I almost died. It was life's most embarrassing phone call to tell her that I had her earrings. If we had been on a tight little island, we would have killed each other by the time it was all over. At the end of the trip, we all went away mad, but now that we've had time to cool off and think back over it, we all really loved it and it wasn't, or shouldn't have been, all that serious. I'd do it again in a minute, knowing everything that I know. And I know a lot."

Katzy and John Mecom came through relatively unscathed. Katzy turns up on best-dressed, best-jeweled, and best-looking lists just often enough to be hated on a yacht. Her shipmates had hair problems, clothes problems, diet problems, and the like. But not Katzy! She was eternally right, wearing the best dress and sporting the best jewels to boot. Katzy had her own problem, which was keeping her volatile husband grounded, so to speak, for the length of *Nefertiti*'s voyage. John Mecom owns the New Orleans Saints football team. The team was playing its little heart out in the all-important pre-season games and John Mecom could never find out if his team had won or lost. He spent maddening hours, whenever he could get ashore, hanging around semi-defunct Spanish or Italian telephones trying to find out how the New Orleans Saints had fared. The score determined his mood.

Marilyn (Jackie) Horne, whose voice thrills Metropolitan Opera goers, and her husband, Henry Lewis, who is the conductor of the New Jersey Symphony Orchestra, didn't make such beautiful music together as *Nefertiti* steamed her way toward the end of her voyage. Although it was not apparent to any of the others at the time, there were some seams bursting in the Lewis marriage. As a matter of fact, the Lewises seemed the calmest and most rational pair aboard, and when small personality-storms would blow up, Jackie and Henry were the ruffled-feather smoothers. Maybe they should have stayed on the yacht. At the end of the cruise, they had been ashore for about twenty minutes when they announced that their marriage, as well as their vacation, was over.

Another casualty of the trip was Evonne Severinsen, then married to "Doc" Severinsen of Johnny Carson fame. She went to sea a married lady and came ashore a separated one. They say "the wife is the last to know" and Evonne Severinsen did not know she was about to become an ex-wife. It will be a long time before she sets foot on a yacht again, leaving a lover or a husband on dry land.

§

"Well," said Farol Seretean, "I go along with Kay. If I had it to do all over, I would do it all over. I'm sorry about Jackie and Henry's marriage, and Evonne Severinsen's separation. People on a yacht get carried away and get in all sorts of trouble, almost as if they were looking for it. But I think being on *Nefertiti* brought the troubles to a head; certainly they did not start while we were aboard.

"The best of the *Nefertiti* trip for me was Formentor, in Majorca. None of us knew anything about it. We pulled in there one morning for an hour and stayed three days. Bud is great at that sort of thing. Drop a hat and we stay forever, drop another one and whoosh, off we go to the next place if we don't like the one we're in. But I know I would never want to own a yacht, nor would Bud. It's just not our scene. It's not that I mind paying the price, though. And with *Nefertiti*, we sure did!"

8
Cleopatra's Barge

The only thing Elizabeth Taylor ever waited for in her whole life was the Burton diamond. She waited for it, restlessly, on her yacht *Kalizma*, which was moored in the port at Monte Carlo. She was wearing a pale blue caftan with a neckline cut to her waist. Her hair was drawn back into a simple knot at the nape of her neck. She was barefoot.

Elizabeth, who has kept everyone she has ever known or ever worked for waiting—sometimes for years—could not wait to get her mitts on her new 69.4-carat diamond. It finally arrived, just the way a rock that size should arrive—by plane, helicopter, boat, police escort, and two guards armed with machine guns.

The Burton diamond, as it has come to be known, was escorted from New York by two bag men from Cartier. All three of them arrived at the Nice airport in the late afternoon. The security surrounding them suggested either sophisticated Soviet methods or the kind of arrangements usually made for visiting kings or heads of state. First, they were flown off the Nice airstrip by helicopter, landing a quarter of an hour later on the helicopter pad at the Hôtel de Paris in Monte Carlo. Then, with armed guards surrounding them, the Cartier men walked down the flight of wide steps that lead from the landing pad to the boat dock on the sea, where a Monegasque police patrol boat awaited them.

The object was to avoid getting anywhere near the roads, for Cartier and the Monte Carlo police felt that the whole operation would be safer if carried out by sea. If you know Monte Carlo, you remember that it is just a hop, skip, and a jump from the Hôtel de Paris to the port, by land or by sea. The police boat, carrying the machine-gun laden guards, the Cartier men, and the huge, blue-white stone, turned on its sirens, and, although it was not quite dark, the patrol light probed every nook and cranny as they came into the harbor. Keeping a low profile obviously was not part of the security plan. It was quite a sight.

Aboard *Kalizma*, all was chaos. The children wanted to see the diamond. Richard Burton wanted another look at his $1,050,000 gift to his wife. The various secretaries, hairdressers, photographers, and the dogs and cats that always accompanied the Burtons were dying for a peek. Everyone rushed to the windows of the main salon when they heard the sirens wailing. Elizabeth couldn't get an eye in edgewise, so she dashed back to her bedroom and watched from her own window as the police boat came alongside. When the two Cartier men were safely aboard, she returned to the main salon and held out her hands for the large black suede box. She opened the box immediately — and there lay the diamond, looped onto a chain of platinum and small diamonds.

"Well, put it on me, put it on me!" she ordered, eyes glittering. *"And hurry up!"* She had done her own hair and chosen the simple dress carefully. Her personal photographer, Gianni Bozzachi, snapped happily away, and everyone ooh'ed and aah'ed. Mama had a new bauble.

When the initial excitement died down, Richard and Elizabeth sent everyone away but the children and had dinner *en famille* aboard *Kalizma*. Elizabeth arranged and rearranged the candles in the dining salon so that the diamond really blazed. For the next few days the diamond was the star. They talked about nothing else, and the only problem was getting it back from Liza Todd, who wanted to sleep with it. Then, as with all of her other jewels, the novelty palled, up it went into the bank vault in Monte Carlo, and the Burtons went back to yachting as usual.

§

Kalizma is yet another example of Elizabeth's impetuous nature. When she wants something, she wants it *now*. Open up the shop, charter the plane, wake up the lawyer, but *get* it — and get it fast. A few years before the diamond episode, Richard and Elizabeth had come to Monte Carlo as guests of their close friends, Princess Grace and Prince Rainier, for one of Princess Grace's benefits. During their visit, Gloria and Loel Guinness invited them to dine aboard their yacht, *Sarina*. Gloria is a perfectionist and *Sarina* is one of her most perfect creations. Elizabeth's eyes opened wider and wider as she saw more of *Sarina*, for she had never suspected that yachting could be like this. "I want one," she said to Richard on the way home. "One what?" he asked. "One yacht," she answered.

The next day they went shopping. *Kalizma* was owned at the time by an Englishman, and her name was *Minona*. She was a good-sized yacht, a little over 140 feet, and she had spacious quarters. There were masses of other yachts available, but Elizabeth never even looked at another one. They bought *Minona* on the spot. Her new name was a combination of the names of their girl children, Kate, Liza, and Maria.

Unlike her new mistress, *Kalizma* was no beauty. She was an old girl then, a really old girl, and she was, and is, ugly. She was built in Scotland in 1906, which means that she was sixty-two years old when the Burtons bought her. People strolling the port, hoping for a glimpse of at least one Burton, would say, *"That* old tub is the *Burton* yacht?"* when told who the inelegant boat belonged to. Even so, *Kalizma* was seaworthy and she had a spaciousness that appealed to Elizabeth. In those days, the easiest and only getaway for Elizabeth and Richard Burton and their children was provided by their yacht. Elizabeth couldn't have cared less about the outside look of the yacht, nor the bridge, nor the engine room. The interior was all that mattered to her and she went at it as if she had been cut off from any form of luxury for years, poor child. When a London interior-decorating firm finished work on *Kalizma*, some six months later, the Burtons had a gilded lily of the highest order.

Expensive paintings seem to be a must on the bigger and better yachts, and Elizabeth had some that make museum curators sit up and take notice. Her uncle, Howard Taylor, owned a gallery in Beverly Hills and had collected paintings for Elizabeth from the time she was a little girl. He bought her a Vlaminck or two, not to mention Van Gogh, Bonnard, Renoir and Vuillard, among others. Elizabeth's collection holds its own with any other collection, and it bests many. She called for ten of her favorites to be sent to *Kalizma*. Elizabeth is known to be casual about the care and feeding of material posessions, and frantic art experts and nervous insurance men arrived with the paintings to see to it that every last one was hermetically sealed under glass before being hung. They also insisted on their being securely bolted to the walls. When the experts finished, a Utrillo hung in the main salon, a Franz Hals in the library, and a delicate Dégas in the master suite. The rest were scattered casually but safely about the ship.

The master suite was worthy of the superstars it sheltered. The curtains and bedspread were made of canary yellow silk, and the rug and walls were white, with a white fur throw rug flung over a chaise lounge in one corner. All the linens were Porthault, patterned with pale yellow and blue polka dots and embroidered with violets, Elizabeth's favorite flower, on their organdy edges.

Chris and Michael Wilding shared a large bedroom on the deck below, and Liza and Maria shared another one alongside the boys. The only guest room is almost the size of the master suite. It could sleep four, if necessary, and was normally inhabited by the children's school chums, as Richard and Elizabeth rarely asked even close friends to stay on board for long. All in all, the yacht slept sixteen comfortably, although there were seldom more than seven sleep-in's aboard, made up of Elizabeth, Richard, and the five children. It was a family yacht, and it was the only place where Richard and Elizabeth were ever alone together for any length of time. They sought peace and quiet, and on *Kalizma* they got it. The library was Richard's pride and joy. "Richard would rather read a book than have a drink, and *that's* saying something," Elizabeth remarked. Two soft, comfortable couches also double as beds in the library.

The Burtons poured approximately two million dollars into *Kalizma*. She carried a crew of eleven, and as an added insurance of privacy, only the captain and the chef spoke any English. When hired, each captain was bonded not to sell gossip or stories to the press, and they didn't. Nevertheless, Richard fired two captains in his time. Although he was nowhere near as fond of *Kalizma* as Elizabeth was, Richard handled all problems and saw to it that they were never made known to Elizabeth.

Because of the Burtons' fear of kidnapping, armed robbery, more publicity, or invasion of privacy, the captain was never told in advance what their destination was—if indeed *they* knew where they were going. They fought tooth and nail about destinations, with Elizabeth eventually giving way to wherever Richard wanted to go. "All right, all right, *all right* already!" she would rage, throwing in four-letter word descriptions of the Welsh in general. "We will *go* to Portofino, as you like, *dear*, even though they do suspect cholera there." And to Portofino they would go.

When the Burton group boarded *Kalizma*, the captain would have had no more than a few days' warning, so he kept the yacht almost completely provisioned for ten days to two weeks of cruising. *Kalizma* was ready to depart as soon as the weather was fair. The minute they boarded, and as soon as they were out of the harbor, the captain would be told to head to Majorca or Capri, or wherever they had decided to go. This in no way reflected on their trust in the captain; it was simply easier to keep their destination secret. If you don't know where you are going, you cannot tell anybody, and that way they avoided the prying eyes of cameras and reporters that turned up wherever they went and converged on them in swarms.

Many times they would just cruise along the coast of France or Italy, stopping in small ports for lunch or dinner. The two flamboyant film stars, with two young boys, three girls, four cats, seven dogs, and the captain and crew, spent many happy hours aboard, and enjoyed their rare moments of privacy. Everyone wore slacks and cotton shirts or bathing suits in the daytime. Elizabeth would slip into something long, comfortable, and weight-concealing at night, usually a caftan, and bedeck herself with some of the less important but nevertheless numerous and magnificent jewels that the insurance company had agreed to let her bring on the yacht.

§

The Burtons' voyages were all in the Mediterranean in the summertime, when the children were out of school. One year, Elizabeth and Richard had to go to England to make a film called *The V.I.P.'s,* but England's six-month quarantine law made it impossible for them to take their menagerie of animals along. "Impossible?" said Elizabeth. "The hell with that. We aren't going anywhere for four months of filming without them. What do we have the yacht for? We'll take it and moor it in the Thames." Which they did. Big yachts tied up at the Tower Bridge near the heart of London, but *Kalizma* was the first one to moor there for any length of time in years, and, naturally, it became an instant tourist attraction. The Burtons lived aboard for almost six months, causing another holocaust of publicity by their mere presence. Their two white Pekinese dogs, the three Yorkies, and a varying number of Abyssinian cats never set foot on English soil, but they had a sensational view of London, and barked and meowed ecstatically when their master and mistress came back aboard after a hard day's work in front of the cameras.

Elizabeth had a favorite game that she often played aboard *Kalizma*. "Bring me my jewels," she would say to one of her male secretaries. "Let's play today." The boxes would be brought and everyone pawed happily through the jewels. Elizabeth would drape Liza and Maria and Kate with hundreds of carats of sapphires and emeralds and corals and turquoises, precious and semi-precious alike, all jumbled together. No one had enough fingers or toes for them all.

One day she put on the fabulous Perigrina pearl that Richard had given her a few months before. Suddenly she grabbed at the chain around her neck. "My God," she said. "The pearl, where is the pearl?" It was gone. A mad scramble ensued, with everyone on their hands and knees searching for it, going over every inch of the deep shaggy carpet, searching in the cushions on the couches and chairs. No pearl. Then Elizabeth screamed, "*Ofi!!!....*" and lunged at the white peke who was contentedly chewing away on the Peregrina and was about to swallow it. "Little bitch," Elizabeth said. "You do have good taste." The jewels went back into *Kalizma's* safe until they could be transported back to the bank vault. When they are taken out of the bank vaults, no matter where, insurance costs run a minimum of a thousand dollars a day. Elizabeth's taste in jewels and games is expensive.

Food has always been important to Elizabeth, although her desire for good old meat-and-potato fare has never changed. Dave Chasen, a dear friend and restaurant owner in Beverly Hills, sent off regular supplies of homemade beef stew and his world-famous chili to *Kalizma*. The wine cellar, if it can be called that on a yacht, was crammed full of Elizabeth's favorite Dom Perignon champagne.

Elizabeth is an ardent—though infrequent—cook. She would decide she couldn't live for ten more minutes without some real American fried chicken, and on would go the apron. Flour and salt and pepper would fly around the galley until the grease started to spatter. Then the famous violet eyes would narrow. "Shit," she would say, now wanting to eat, not cook, and she would yell for Ramon to take over. Mashed potatoes were a must, too, and they were *real* mashed potatoes. Woe be to Ramon if he ever used the packaged variety. Not for Elizabeth. She would roll up her sleeves and pound away, heaping butter and hot milk and salt and pepper onto steaming mounds of freshly mashed potatoes, and trying desperately not to devour them all on the way to the table.

Yachting was a perfect pastime for Elizabeth Taylor. She loves to do nothing, and she loves to talk and eat and drink while she is doing it. Lying in the sun on the top deck was exercise for her. Just getting up there was strenuous work. Elizabeth was fairly athletic when she was younger, but persistent back troubles over the years have made it impossible for her to attempt anything more than an occasional dunk in the most lakelike sea.

§

Friends are her favorite pastime, but Elizabeth and Richard Burton had a highly impersonal circle of "intimate" friends. Those closest to them were the ones who worked for them. Claudye, a pretty French hairdresser who came to Elizabeth from Alexandre in Paris, always had Elizabeth's ear, and so did Claudye's husband, Gianni Bozzachi, a papparazzi-type photographer. He was always on hand, snapping away, although Richard detested him. The makeup men, the wardrobe ladies, the lawyers, the secretaries, and the agents were all part of the close circle surrounding the Burtons, and the loyalty of each one was long proven. Beyond that group, whoever they worked with became close to them, but only until whichever film they were working on was finished. With each new film, a new group of friends would appear.

The Burtons knew everyone, of course, and were invited everywhere. Aristotle Onassis took quite a shine to Mrs. Burton, but the timing was wrong for both, and the friendship cooled considerably when Jackie's last name became Onassis. When Richard made a film in Yugoslavia,

Elizabeth went along, and *Kalizma* was sent for. They struck up quite a friendship with Tito and he took them to Brioni—his private island—on his private yacht. (True to Communist custom, Tito's yacht has a number rather than a name, and is referred to as the "State yacht." Funny thing though—no one uses it but Tito.) In Monte Carlo Princess Grace invited the Burtons to screenings at the palace, and the Rainiers would often pack up their children on *Stalca*, the Rainier yacht, and rendezvous with the Burtons for water-skiing or island picnicking. But the friendships were all, somehow, transitory. It was an out-of-sight, out-of-mind way of living.

When the Burtons parted, everything changed, including the yacht. Somehow it was fitting, and rather sad, that at the end of the summer of '74, Elizabeth chartered *Kalizma* to an old friend who had called her needing help. It was Rex Harrison. He had given up his villa in Portofino, which had been home to him for nearly twenty years, and bought a villa in the south of France. He wanted to move some of his possessions, including some large pieces of furniture, from Portofino to his new place in Cap Ferrat. If Elizabeth would charter the yacht to him, he could load up all the cumbersome objects collected over the years and bring them over by yacht. Elizabeth agreed to the charter and generously sent *Kalizma* from Monte Carlo, charging Rex only for the days from Portofino back to the south of France.

Rex had chartered *Kalizma* before, but this time it was very different. The paintings were gone and in their place were prints. Good prints, but only prints. There were still books in the library, but Richard Burton's books were gone. The Porthault linen was no more; instead, more mundane linens replaced them. The yacht seemed ownerless, although it was still a joint possession of the Burtons.

Rex spent ten days on *Kalizma*. He unloaded everything at his new Cap Ferrat villa, and the last day of his charter he invited about twenty friends for a final summer luncheon on board. There were bouquets of flowers everywhere, and plenty of ice cold champagne for the glamorous group of chums. Gregory Peck and Roger Moore came, with wives and children. Leslie Bricusse brought his wife Evie and son Adam. David Hemmings and Gene Hackman were there. Edmond de Rothschild brought his villa guests, and Simone and Bill Levitt came bringing their group from *La Belle Simone*, which was anchored nearby.

In the main salon there were several large photographs of Elizabeth, wearing pink trousers and shirt, with a printed pink scarf tied about her hair. She was resting comfortably, and smiling happily, in Mr. Henry Wynberg's arms. She had brought her new man aboard earlier in the summer, and left the photographs behind. No foot dragger, Elizabeth, when it comes to men.

It seemed right that Rex was the last person on *Kalizma* before she went back to the yacht broker in Barcelona to be sold. Rex played Caesar to Richard Burton's Antony and Elizabeth Taylor's Cleopatra, fourteen years before in Rome, when the Burton-Taylor romance began its dizzy, dazzling journey across the capitals and watering spots of the world. He was there at the beginning, and here was Caesar himself, in the person of old-friend Rex Harrison, at the end. It wasn't *the* end, of course, but it was the beginning of the end.

9
Mistress to Many Men

Tracing the history of a fine yacht from her origins to her demise is like following the life of a fabulously beautiful woman.

The yacht, like the woman, would be expensive, of course. But she would be durable and changeable, and she would have qualities that would keep you with her long after she had ceased to excite you. She would be yours, but she would belong to others, too. She would satisfy you and soothe you, but there would be times when, by the very fact of her existence, she would drive you to madness—or to bankruptcy. Your would buy her and sell her and, perhaps, want to buy her again someday. In the end, when you thought about her, you would know more about yourself, and, hopefully, because you cared about her, you would take care of her.

Maid Marion was born in Southampton, England, in

1938, the summer before the Second World War. She was named before she came into being by her mentor and benefactor, Sir Harold Bowden. Sir Harold's fortune came from metal cables, which provided him with more than enough money to indulge himself in exactly the yacht that he wanted. He christened her *Maid Marion* for the lovely lady who had intrigued Robin Hood, and who, though the romance was turbulent, loved him until she died.

Maid Marions's passports are infinite. She has been English, Indochinese, Italian, American, and Canadian. Now, toward the end of her life, she has been an old man's darling twice. Her last two owners died, loving her still, but leaving her in litigation that has kept her resting in Southampton, from whence she came, since early in the seventies. *Maid Marion* is growing old without her Robin Hood.

Unlike Robin Hood's lady, this *Maid Marion* cost a packet. She was designed and built by Camper & Nicholsons, the great yacht builders in England, and she went proudly into the water in May of 1938, after more than two years' building. Her final cost when she was turned over to Sir Harold came to £65,000, which in those days was approximately $325,000.

One of her most unusual features was the absence of a traditional master suite. In a yacht 173 feet long, with seven cabins for sleeping, there was no grandiose, kingly, bigger-and-better-than-the-rest-of-them bed, bath, and dressing room combination. The five double cabins were all more or less the same size, and the two singles were plenty spacious. That's a great quality for a present-day charter yacht to have, but for a yacht conceived and built by a monarchy-minded titled Englishman who was bound to be a snob, it was an enigma.

British snobbery won out over British reticence when it came to the yacht's maiden voyage. Sir Harold and *Maid Marion* beat it to the Mediterranean as fast as the two of them could get there so everyone could see the biggest and newest yacht that money could buy. Sir Harold tootled around to as many ports as he could that first summer, lingering longest in Cannes, the bay of Villefranche, and Monte Carlo. He showed her off proudly to his seagoing and shorebound friends.

The last week in August found them at Cowes on the Isle of Wight, the fountainhead of English yachting and home of the Royal Yacht Squadron. Cowes Week is a must to the best yachting snobs, status-seekers, and sailors, all the way from able-bodied seamen to admirals. The Cowes folk are the epitome of yachting, even though they are a pretty stuffy bunch of sailing aristocrats. Prince Philip is there every year with *Britannia*, and even the Queen shows up once in a while.

Sir Harold was sufficiently confident of *Maid Marion's* prowess to preen with her at Cowes that first summer. She was faultless, and he was crazy about her. She came through with flying colors. When she went back to Camper & Nicholsons' shipyard in early September, there was some routine work to be done but, generally speaking, she was perfect. Quite a lady, *Maid Marion* was.

Maid Marion was ready and waiting for Sir Harold the following June, and she made her graceful way around the Med once more and returned to Cowes in August, as she had the summer before. But the summer of 1939 had an entirely different flavor, for the coming war occupied everyone's thoughts. There was apprehension in the air because British yachtsmen already felt that a world was ending, and they were right. The mood at Cowes was showoff, on the surface. Worries were hidden by British bravado, the glorious weather, and the beauty of the yachts.

Camper & Nicholsons' great and beloved designer, Charlie Nicholson, dashed about on more than a dozen yachts of his own design, including *Maid Marion*. The yachting world never saw anything like that August week at Cowes ever again. The great time of yachting, when a man could build and enjoy the privileges of a fine yacht, began at the end of the Kaiser's war in 1918, and ended in September 1939 with the start of Hitler's war. It was a good-bye to a beautiful era. When Cowes Week was over, *Maid Marion* went back to her home yard in Southampton, and within a few short weeks she was at war.

C H R I S T I N
Y. C. M.

The two superstars of the yachting world, Aristotle S. Onassis and Jacqueline Kennedy, aboard *Christina*, Onassis' favorite material possession. *Sygma*

Jacqueline Kennedy, widow of U.S. President John F. Kennedy, with her two children, John (holding her hand) and Caroline (following), arriving at the Greek island Skorpios, owned by Aristotle Onassis, for Mrs. Kennedy's marriage to Onassis. In the background can be seen Onassis' yacht, *Christina. Camera Press Ltd.*

Aristotle Onassis' most famous and apprecia-
tive guest on board *Christina* was Winston
Churchill. Churchill cruised each summer and
winter with Onassis and reputedly loved the
yacht as much as Onassis did. In Churchill's
waning years, he was fed and read to by Onassis.
Here he sits with the ever-present cigar. Maria
Callas and her husband, Giovanni Meneghini,
were guests that summer; the following summer
Callas was aboard alone.

United Press International

The bar stools of *Christina*, covered with whale
scrotums, caused quite a conversational ripple
with the international set. Whale teeth were
used as foot rests, and when Stavros Niarchos
built his yacht *Atlantis*, his bar stools too were

The afterdeck of *Christina*, seen here in the harbor of Monte Carlo, has a mosaic dance floor that can be lowered to become the floor of a swimming pool. Winston Churchill and Onassis had a favorite game of seating themselves in two armchairs on the bottom of the waterless pool while the engineer worked the hydraulic lift to elevator them up and down. The game was fun until Churchill got stuck midway one day, causing Onassis to curse the engineer until the great man was brought successfully to the surface.

Above: *United Press International,*
right: *Paris Match*

Aristotle Onassis' Siena marble bathroom aboard *Christina* was the favorite attraction of the famous yacht. It was copied from one belonging to King Minos of Crete, centuries before, and was the scene of some famous parties in Onassis' heyday. *Paris Match*

Stavros Niarchos stands on the deck of his gigantic *Atlantis* in the harbor of Monte Carlo. When he first brought her into the harbor and berthed her near the entrance, she blocked the view of half the yachts in the harbor, and earned the anger of the other yacht owners, who disparagingly referred to her as "the cruise ship."

Sygma

Nedenia Hutton and her mother, Mrs. Edward F. Hutton, in matching sarongs and leis, cruised through Hawaiian waters on *Hussar*. All changed their names. Nedenia grew up to be known as actress Dina Merrill; Marjorie Hutton married several times and finally reverted to her original name, Marjorie Post. When she and Edward F. Hutton divorced, she kept *Hussar*, painted her black hull white, and renamed her *Sea Cloud*.

From the private collection of Dina Merrill

Actress Dina Merrill spent more than six months of each year cruising on her mother's and father's great sailing bark, *Hussar*, which became *Sea Cloud* when her parents were divorced. Here, Dina rides on the back of Jumbo, a giant sea turtle the Hutton's adopted in the Galapagos Islands, and who became the ship mascot. Coiled behind Dina is some of the eight-and-a-half miles of rope needed to set *Sea Cloud*'s sails.

From the private collection of Dina Merrill

The royal yacht *Britannia* in Brisbane, Australia, on a royal cruise that keeps the Queen busy and gives rise to complaints from British taxpayers, who support *Britannia* to the tune of more than one million dollars a year.

Camera Press Ltd. (Brenda Judge)

Lady Yule built *Nahlin* and chartered it to Edward VIII for a romantic cruise along the Yugoslavian coast and through the Greek Islands. When it was over, the King of England abdicated and married twice-divorced Mrs. Wallis Simpson, showing the power of a ship-

. P. Morgan built four yachts named *Corsair*, all of them among the most beautiful and famous of American yachts. When Morgan was asked how much it cost to maintain a yacht, he delivered the most famous line in yachting with his reply, "If you have to ask, you can't afford it."

Above and right: *United Press International*

William J. Levitt's 227-foot *La Belle Simone*, lit up at dusk in Puerto Jose Banus in Marbella, Spain. She was the largest yacht ever to maneuver into the harbor, yet, as can be seen in the photograph, her afterdeck was almost stubby looking. The following summer, Levitt added eighteen feet to her stern to improve her stabilization and not, as rumor had it, to make her longer than Charles Revson's *Ultima II*.

From the collection of Nancy Holmes

Mr. and Mrs. William J. Levitt, with their yacht, *La Belle Simone*, named after Mrs. Levitt, in the background. *Town and Country*

Cleo and John von Neumann symbolize the young world of yachting. *Cochise,* their fifth Baglietto, cruises at forty-one knots and is crewed only by a captain and one sailor. John von Neumann trades in his speedy yachts every two years for a new model.

Above and left:
From the collection of Nancy Holmes

Elizabeth Taylor and Richard Burton, seen here with daughter Liza Todd, spent happy and private hours aboard *Kalizma* until one of their

Errol Flynn's first yacht, *Sirocco*, was like an evil wind to him, but his black schooner, *Zaca*, gave him the most pleasurable hours of his life. Flynn was a true sailor. His years of residence in Jamaica came about when he was blown into an exquisite Jamaican bay on the fringes of a hurricane. Flynn lived aboard *Zaca* for the last four years of his life.

United Press International

Chartering *Nefertiti* for two weeks cost Bud and Farol Seretean a lot of money. It cost several of their guests much more, and the French chef nearly lost his mind preparing diet food until the Sereteans relented and allowed him to produce his soufflés and sauces.

Author and yacht-lover Nancy Holmes at the Balboa Bay Club in Newport Beach, California, would like to live aboard a one-hundred foot power yacht with a crew of five, roaming the world and never having to pack or unpack a suitcase again. *Douglas Kirkland*

Mexican washing-machine millionaire Ramon Carlin, a part-time sailor, took some of his family on a 'round-the-world race which he won—to the surprise of everyone except his experienced and knowledgeable crew. "This will be a quarter-of-a-million-dollar joyride for me," he predicted, and then spent a half million dollars enjoying himself.

United Press International

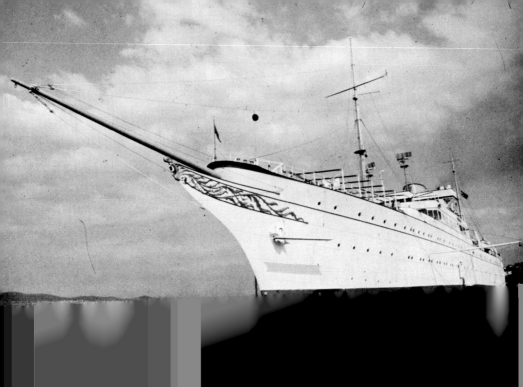

One of the guest staterooms on *Savarona III*. Although old-fashioned by today's standards, the years between the two World Wars produced an era of luxury yachting the world will never see again. *From the collection of Nancy Holmes*

Morgan Wells was commissioned by Mr. and Mrs. Richard Cadwallader to do the interiors of *Savarona III*. He spent a year in Paris ordering each and every piece of furniture, with Louis XIV, XV, and XVI reproductions predominant and safe from sea air. The green hall led to a marble stairway, graced with ornamental iron balustrades.

From the collection of Nancy Holmes

Monte Carlo harbor on a summer night is one
of the great glamour places of the world. In
the foreground, Aristotle Onassis' *Christina* is
"dressed" with her myriad strings of light.
Ulli Skoruppa, Camera Press Ltd.

Overleaf: Charles Revson cruised for seven
summers in the Mediterranean and seven summers in the Caribbean and Pacific, only to find
that his guests were unappreciative of much
of the effort he made for them. Still, *Ultima II*
was Revson's favorite status symbol and the
one that gave him the most pleasure.
Robert Huntzinger

The opening salvos of September 1939 had hardly died down before every large motor yacht in England was called up on war service. They were chartered out to the Admiralty, and it had nothing to do with whether an owner wanted to charter his yacht or not. It was a matter of pure patriotism and desperate need. The Admiralty paid to charter British yachts from the largest to the smallest. They were, in actuality, buying a small navy for war service. It took months before an Admiralty office could be established in Southampton, and until then, Camper & Nicholsons took on the responsibility for the yachts in their own yard and did the work for the Admiralty. The company actually engaged naval crews, gave them their rank, sent them to get uniforms and supplies, and paid them. The shipyard, just like every other shipyard in the United Kingdom, became an instant branch of the Admiralty.

The beautiful yachts were stripped of their luxurious trappings, painted gray, numbered, and fitted out primarily for anti-submarine or escort duty. *Maid Marion* became a gunboat. Before Christmas, she was off to the South Pacific, where she spent five years in action. When she was at last released in 1944, the war effort had finally produced the ships necessary to do what *Maid Marion* had been doing for over four years. No longer useful, and certainly no longer new and perfect, she limped back to England, wounded and tired, but still very much afloat.

The policy of the Admiralty, when yachts that had been on war service returned to England, was to offer them back to their owners at a value set by a surveyor. *Maid Marion* was offered back to Sir Harold Bowden for £27,000. He had been down to see her and had gone all over her. The gray, gun-laden, beat-up war ship that she now was showed not even a remnant of his beloved *Maid Marion.* She had served thousands of men safely, and hundreds of them had written Sir Harold, praising her seaworthiness and her behavior in emergency. Sir Harold was impressed, but *Maid Marion* was no longer his pristine queen of the sea; she was a pockmarked and damaged lady and he no longer had any desire to keep her. He refused the offer to buy her back.

§

Maid Marion's next owner was another Englishman named Augustus J. Newman. Gus had watched *Maid Marion* in the south of France as she cruised through her two shake-down summers before the war. He had the keen and canny eye of a shrewd yachtsman, he knew Sir Harold Bowden, he knew *Maid Marion* even better, and the minute he learned that Sir Harold had turned her down, Gus Newman decided to buy her.

He bought her early in 1945, paying the £27,000 asked for her. It was condiberably less than she had cost to build, obviously, but Gus spent an additional £80,000 re-fitting her. The war-weary yacht was a mess. There were deep gun-emplacement trenches in her decks, causing a major repair problem. However, Gus Newman was living in Bournemouth at the time, and he had noticed an old wreck lying off the nearby island of Brownsea. When the tide allowed, Gus inspected the wreck and discovered that, fortunately, her teak decks were still in good condition. He then got permission from the Commissioner of Wrecks to rip off her undamaged decks and use them on *Maid Marion*. It was a difficult job, since the workmen never had more than an hour a day, during low tide, to strip the wreck. But they succeeded, and soon *Maid Marion*'s past beauty was restored.

Many of *Maid Marion*'s luxurious belongings that had been stored in Southampton during the war were lost when more than two-thirds of the town was flattened by bombs. But Gus bought back the few pieces of her former furnishings that had survived and he fitted her out as closely as possible to her original, luxurious condition. He added some smashing antiques of his own. By the begin-ning of 1946, the yacht was in great shape again and ready for a shakedown cruise to Scandinavia. Later in the sum-mer she would go back to Monte Carlo once more, bearing her new owner and her new name.

Her new name was *Jagusy*. Gus combined the names of his wife, Jan, his mother, Lucy, and his father's and his own name, Augustus. She flew the colors of the Royal Thames Yacht Club, as before, and she had a superb crew of twenty-four, all seasoned hands and all delirious with the pleasure of peacetime yachting after a long, filthy war. *Jagusy* was a happy ship.

In the late autumn of 1948, two years after Gus had finally gotten her back in perfect condition and was enjoying her to the fullest, the British Foreign Office called on him.

"They wanted to know if I wanted to sell her," he said indignantly. Just like that, like a bolt out of the blue. Why in the world would I want to sell her? I asked them. It took me nine months to rebuild her, and a vast amount of money and time. 'She's a fine yacht and I have no desire to part with her. Thank you very much, but no.' That was the end of it for awhile, but a few months later the same man from the Foreign Office called me again and asked if he could come in and have a drink that afternoon, which, naturally, I agreed to. This time he brought another chap with him. I had no idea what they wanted, and it never occurred to me that they were still thinking about *Jagusy*. But they were. And this time, they meant to have her.

"The other man, it turned out, was a representative of Emperor Bao Dai, who was the Emperor of Indo-China. The French were going to present the Emperor with a yacht as a symbol of their esteem. The Emperor wasn't going to be given just any old yacht, so he had sent his own representative to watch what they were up to and to be sure that the new yacht was suitable to his imperial stature. There were no yachts of the size or quality of *Jagusy* available in France then. It was much too soon after the war, and the French have never built yachts as we did in Britain. The yacht they really wanted was *Jagusy*, and that was why they made the first offer to me. When I refused, they looked around, but nothing good enough for the Emperor had turned up. They were determined to have *Jagusy*."

Gus Newman was nonplussed and annoyed. "When

a representative of your King or Queen calls on you, wanting or needing something of yours, it is very difficult to turn him down. Oh, I could have, but not with good conscience. So I agreed to sell her for just what she had cost me overall, but I wanted an agreement that I could buy her back for the same price if the Emperor tired of her."

Gus sold *Jagusy*. She was duly presented to Nguyen Vinh Thuy Bao Dai, Emperor of Indo-China, puppet and long-time pawn of the French. Born in 1912, Bao Dai was crowned Emperor in 1928 when he was sixteen years old. He was the last in a line that had ruled for more than 150 years in Indo-China, Vietnam, or whatever history is calling that tragic geography now. He ruled until 1945, but only in a manner of speaking. The French, the Japanese, and Ho Chi Minh had a hand in, too. When he abdicated at thirty-three, both by suggestion and persuasion, he was given the puppet title of High-Chancellor, ostensibly presiding in Hanoi. In 1948 the French turned up with another title for him, this time Chief of Staff, but Chief of Staff of what? Both the title and the yacht were delivered to him for the same reason. To get him away from it all—and that was not too difficult a task. Bao Dai loved Vietnam, France, and the yachting life, and now he was handed all three on a French silver platter. *Maid Marion*, ex-*Jagusy*, was renamed *Huong Giang*. That mouthful of name means "River Perfume" in Vietnamese, and it is the name of the river that flows through Hué, the ancient capital of Vietnam and Bao Dai's sometime home.

Emperors will be emperors and playboys will be playboys, and the twain quite often meet. Bao Dai was a part-time participant as both, and he had his contradictions in both. On the one hand, he was a family man, with a wife, two sons, and three daughters always near him. On the other hand, he was a hunter, a gambler, and a womanizer. He also had a very important something extra. About a ton of dough. He had a villa in Cannes and the most important title on the Riviera. How many emperors have you met wandering around loose lately—rich or poor? We can hardly find those kind anymore.

Bao Dai's inclinations leaned toward fast Italian cars, classical Spanish guitar playing, and yachts. He could afford to indulge in all three, and he did. He didn't have to indulge much in refitting *Huong Giang*, though, for she needed hardly any changes to accommodate her royal inhabitant. When she took her first trip out to Saigon, air conditioning was added, which was almost unheard of on yachts then, but a must in Indo-China at any time of year. To this day, the only obvious sign of Vietnamese occupancy is a small plaque in the engine room which reads, "In case of trouble with the air conditioning, please telephone Saigon 232." Try that number the next time you're out there.

One other change was a secret escape passage from Bao Dai's private quarters. Being a canny fellow, he had the back wall of his closet hinged and made into a clandestine passageway to the adjoining stateroom, which he used as an office. From there he could slip out on deck and disappear. Even emperors, or especially emperors, need getaways.

Bao Dai lived like a king, as an emperor should, from 1928 until 1945, when the French and Indo-Chinese drama began to draw to a close. He was voted out of power at the Geneva Conference. He continued to spend half the year in France and the other half in Vietnam with his ministers and mandarins still around him, plying his way back and forth twice a year on his 173-foot toy, the French expression of gratitude for all that he had done for them and a lot that he had not. Bao Dai loved *Huong Giang* and even used her as his official office and address when he was in Vietnam. He began to keep pretty much to himself, which was unusual, but his romance with the French was ending. Bao Dai and the French had gotten rich together, but those days finished for both with the French withdrawal from Vietnam, and the relationship between the two deteriorated rapidly.

Bao Dai felt that he had been used by the French, which he had, and the French were quick to resent his attitude, which they would. His insults to the French proved expensive. On one occasion he deliberately bathed nude in the river—a highly insulting Vietnamese way to show his contempt for French troops and their wives. (That picture could have been the first Imperial centerfold. Have you ever seen a naked emperor?)

But the French had their answer to the surly conduct of the Emperor. Having given him *Huong Giang*, they now took her away. It was so easy: they simply stopped paying *Huong Giang's* bills. Bao Dai's expensive tastes hadn't changed but, alas, his income had, and not even he could cover the yacht's bills now. In 1956 *Huong Giang* was impounded for debts in Villefranche. Salaries, dockage charges, maintenance, food and drink bills were all outstanding. *Huong Giang* had fallen upon hard times, and now she was up for grabs again. Bao Dai went to Paris to live, and *Huong Giang* went on the block.

§

Our mistress's next master was an Italian gentleman named Ravano, a shipowner from Genoa who was based in Monte Carlo. He probably got her for a Genoese love song or two by simply paying off her debts. *Maid Marion* was never a bargain yacht, but if ever she went for a bargain price, it was when Ravano bought her. Whatever he paid for her (and her price was not disclosed), it was only a fraction of the more than half million dollars that he sold her for five years later.

Under Ravano's ownership, *Maid Marion* added *Running Eagle II* to her list of names. Papa Ravano had once owned an American merchant ship called *Running Eagle*, which had been in an accident at sea during a horrific storm, and although Ravano had given up hope for her, she managed to limp safely back into port. Her name became lucky to him; but luck or no luck, why in the world a social-climbing Italian would name a glamorous yacht *Running Eagle* defies comprehension. *Huong Giang* was difficult enough, but it was at least in the language of her owner. *Running Eagle* sounds like the kind of Indians that Custer would have preferred, rather than the name of 173 feet full of seagoing elegance.

The Ravanos kept *Running Eagle II* in the Med and turned her into a big Italian family yacht, filled with Ravano's nine sons. Again, no structural changes were necessary, her *100A1 rating remained intact, and as always, she seemed to adapt herself to her owner's needs. Ravano provided her with some tapestry landscapes that still cover the walls of the dining salon, but he came up short in appreciation of a small part of her past. Under Bao Dai, the name plates that graced her bow were exquisite carved wood and metal talismans, painted meticulously in reds and greens, spelling out her name in Vietnamese. They were *objets d'art* in their own right. Elvin, the Swedish engineer who has been with the ship since she was first launched, remembers them being callously thrown overboard in Genoa, where he tried to retrieve them, to no avail.

Five years later, Ravano found a new buyer for *Running Eagle II*. He made a packet from the sale. *Maid Marion, Jagusy, Huong Giang, Running Eagle II* was heading for a new man.

The fifth time around, the yacht's new owner was an American who not only was Somebody, but was an accomplished and experienced yachtsman as well. Once more, she became a queen of the seas. Julius Fleischmann, one of the heirs to the yeast fortune, had been a yacht-owner for many years, was a member of the New York Yacht Club and a well-adjusted, intelligent millionaire. He removed his new yacht from the European scene for the first time in her life. Nassau became her home port, and her official owner was a Bahamian corporation.

Her new name was *Camargo*. For the second time in her life, her name had romantic implications. Maid Marion was a nice girl from Nottingham, but La Camargue was an even more fascinating figure in history. She was a Spanish dancer named Camargo who became a mistress of the multi-mistressed Louis IV. As a dancer, she caught the fancy of the French as well as the French king, and everyone in Paris knew her as La Camargue. "Junkie" Fleischmann named all of his yachts *Camargo*, and this was his fifth. Junkie preferred the Spanish to the French. Ravano was paid $600,000 for *Camargo V*—probably more than

Louis IV ever put out for La Camargue—and immediately a lot more was poured into her. Dorette and Junkie Fleischmann completely redid the interior, furnishing her with beautiful antiques and paintings and books, giving her the mood and look of a comfortable English country home.

Camargo IV's fuel capacity had been too small to make an Atlantic crossing but *Camargo V* could easily make the trip. Seasoned yachtsmen keep expanding their horizons. The Fleischmanns wanted to wander around Europe as well as the Bahamas, and wanted to be able to cross the Atlantic without even having to breathe deeply. *Camargo V* could, and did, twice a year. She was no sooner refurnished than the Fleischmanns lit out for Europe to spend a summer cruising through the Greek islands and the Adriatic.

It was the first time they made the trip on their own yacht, rather than chartering in Europe, and they were able to take along numerous children and innumerable friends. *Camargo V*'s spacious accommodations provided total comfort for twelve guests and there was rarely a cool bed aboard. Dorette Fleischmann liked a full table at every meal and the dining room always played to capacity, at sea or in port.

In Athens, Constantine Nicoludis, an Oxford-educated Greek of wild intellectual capacity and an even wilder sense of humor, joined the Fleischmann ménage as a tutor. Junkie knew that a man who made history come alive and made you laugh at the same time was a valuable asset, and Constantine Nicoludis was that man. Half the yachting world straggles around looking glorious history right in the eye, and for all they know, they could be in Trenton, New Jersey. Constantine Nicoludis owns an internationally established yacht-chartering agency in Athens and he has made both yachting and history a pleasure to a breathtaking Blue Book of beautiful people. The Duchess of Windsor learned a thing or two from him, Mary Lou and Sonny Whitney are rarely seen in Greek waters without him, and Philadelphia socialite Henry McIlhenny has first call on Constantine each summer.

Camargo V was used, loved, cared for, and never empty during the Fleischmann reign. The sociable Fleischmanns ran such a full house that they needed a minimum crew of eighteen to keep up with their guests. Frequently, Dorette would even hire extra domestic help for the summer without mentioning it to the captain. When he was asked once how many crew members he had, he looked around vaguely and said, "I forget right now."

In October of 1968, Junkie Fleischmann died. Dorette had no desire to keep the yacht without her husband. *Camargo V* was about to gain yet another master, this one her last — perhaps.

§

In June 1969 the Fleischmann estate sold *Camargo V* to John F. Eaton, a Canadian. The Fleischmanns and the Eatons did not know each other but they were cut from the same cloth. John Eaton paid $600,000 for *Camargo V*, the same price Junkie had paid to Ravano. This price bought Mr. Eaton much more than it had Mr. Fleishmann, as far as interior furnishing is concerned, but it was still a lot of money for an old girl of thirty-one.

John Eaton had taken a close look at *Camargo* before buying her. *Maid Marion*, ex-*Jagusy*, ex-*Huong Giang*, ex-*Running Eagle*, ex-*Camargo V*, now became *Chimon*, which means "the biggest canoe" to the American Indian. The new name had scarcely been painted on when Eaton decided he should have taken a closer look before purchasing her. He sent her back to Southampton to the Camper & Nicholsons yard for a refit, and there all hell broke loose. *Chimon* needed more than a major refit. She needed to be built anew. She was literally coming apart at the seams.

Eaton proposed a question to Lloyd's insurance firm. Just what good is it to have a *100A1 rating if it doesn't mean any more than the paper it's written on? Many a yachtsman turns apoplectic on this subject, for a rating does not keep a yacht afloat. Eaton started out, as the owner of his "biggest canoe," a very angry man. He went so far as to demand his money back from the Fleischmann estate, but they were no more responsible for the gradual deterioration of the yacht than he was, and both sides knew it. Moreover, both parties should have been informed by insurance or inspection officers of her true condition, but neither the Fleischmann estate nor John F. Eaton had been informed of anything.

The Fleischmann-Eaton interests prevailed upon both the insurers and builders to pay for the building of a practically new yacht, but not before a lot of hooting and hollering had gone on. Originally, they had agreed to share the costs of refitting, but when they discovered what rotten condition the old girl was really in, they got hot under the collar and demanded their rights. The smoke has still not cleared. Rebuilding cost far more than Eaton had paid to buy her. Who was to pay what to whom made everyone miserable except the lawyers. In the midst of the whole mess, John Eaton died. He had never taken a trip on *Chimon*.

And so, for five years, *Chimon* has been berthed in Southampton, where she was born. Elvin, her engineer, is still with her. She is almost as good as new now, ship-shape, expensive, still in litigation — and for sale.

Except for one tiny ray of hope, her future is uncertain. Sir Frank Bowden, son of her original owner, has watched and waited, just as Gus Newman did. He has been to see her in Southampton and has expressed more than just a sentimental interest in her.

Wouldn't it be lovely if a Bowden bought her back and cared for her again, after all these years? Then she would be *Maid Marion* once more, and her story would have come full circle.

10
The Five Hundred Thousand Dollar Joy Ride

There is nothing, absolutely nothing, involving any form of yachting that is not nice and expensive, right down to the toothpicks. Chartering? That's nice. You have the fun and the owner pays the upkeep. Owning? That's fun, too, but as someone once said, a yacht is "a hole in the water entirely surrounded by wood into which you pour money." Racing? A sleek little racer, even one that looks more like a Ford than a Ferrari, can set you back hundreds of thousands of dollars. And as for around the world racing, that's a form of yachting that really makes you a big spender.

A happy-go-lucky Mexican named Ramon Carlin took a crack at racing not long ago. He showed style, flair, courage, and a seemingly endlessly overstuffed wallet when he bought a standard yacht and entered a British race around the world.

Ramon Carlin, who had made a huge fortune manufacturing washing machines in Mexico, indisputably confirmed the laudable concept that all play and no work is a very good way to win. At least, that's the way it worked out this time. In the same race, an unbelievably serious, experienced Scottish yachtsman named Chay Blyth proved conclusively not only that all work and no play makes Jack a dull boy, but that it can also make him a loser.

Carlin pulled the sea rug right out from under Chay Blyth and a number of other first-rate, hard-core sailors. He won the toughest race in Class One Ocean Racing, a class that he had never entered before, and one that makes most people shudder at the thought. The race, sponsored by Whitbread and by England's famous newspaper *The Observer*, takes a minimum of seven months and covers a distance of over 27,000 miles. It's hardly a lark, but you'd never guess that by Carlin. He took a standard boat, a newly assembled crew, numerous members of his family, a big smile, and a half million dollars and away he went, loaded with tequila and tamales for all. And he won. *That* is winning.

At the risk of ignoring some of the finest and best-known sailors in the world of yacht racing, the story of Chay Blyth and Ramon Carlin deserves special attention, for the competitive attitudes of the dour and tough Scotsman and the merry little Mexican are a fascinating study in contrasts. Carlin's extravagances and Blyth's frugalities should have resulted in victory for Blyth. After all, Carlin's unusual frivolities could have sunk him. Sailors, particularly those competing in racing as tough as this, are *supposed* to be tough and hard and trained and Spartan. They're supposed to be like Chay Blyth. Clear eyeballs. Clear heads. Stomach muscles like Muhammad Ali's.

The seventeen boats in the first London *Observer* Round-the-World Race left Portsmouth, England, in September of 1972, not to return until after seven months of hard sailing. Prince Philip honored the occasion with a send-off letter saying, in part, "All sorts of surprising and unexpected things are bound to happen and I am sure the Race Committee will have to give decisions on some very original problems." Right you were, Mr. Prince. He went on to say, "I have little doubt that it will be a great success—particularly for those who finish." Ominous line, eh? Seventeen boats entered, fourteen finished, and three men drowned. As for the success stories, at least one girl got married and the winning yacht was navigated by a woman.

§

Chay Blyth is a real toughie, the kind who should have been a winner in *any* race. He had sailed around the world once before, all by himself—and deliberately going the wrong way. He had also rowed the Atlantic in a twenty-foot dory with John Ridgway. It took the two of them ninety-two days to cover the three thousand miles of Atlantic Ocean from Cape Cod to Galway, but to them it was a breeze. Blyth, having achieved a fame for toughness, was backed in the *Observer* race by "Union Jack" Hayward, one of Britain's richest patriots. Blyth was provided with a specially designed 72-foot ketch, *Great Britain II*, which cost one whale of a lot more than Ramon Carlin's *Sayula II*. Carlin's boat was a normal production model ketch and eight feet shorter than *Great Britain II*.

Chay Blyth's problem was being too tough. It was all work and no play with him. His fierce patriotism and Spartan disciplinarianism stemmed from a contempt for any member of the upper-class yachting set. Rich or poor, they were dismissed as "a bunch of harbor stallions." In that attitude lay the seeds of his defeat.

Blyth was an ex-paratrooper. When he decided to compete in the *Observer* Race, he went pounding right back up to Scotland and whistled for his paratrooper pals. Three hundred of them came out of the woods, and Chay started to work them over. His experience told him that the most important ingredient on a seven-month-long racing voyage was not seamanship but compatibility. "You can always teach someone to sail," he said before the race, "but you can't teach them to get along with each other." True enough. Putting people together on a boat is more dangerous than a mine field at midnight. But did Chay Blyth think he had discovered something that no one else knew? Any millionaire yachtsman could have told him that.

Chay narrowed the number of prospective crew members down to fourteen. It was easy. They dropped like flies when he put them through some of the compatibility and endurance contests he had carefully devised. All of them were isolated from outsiders for long periods of time. They went on grueling route marches. The food and drink were exceptional: curry and water, then curry and water again, before or after charging through the hills of Scotland. What fun!

Meanwhile, back at the washing machine factory, Ramon Carlin was having a ball. He was busy making arrangements for as many as possible of his eight children and six grandchildren to greet him on the quaysides of the several stops around the world. His wife, one son, and two nephews would be with him for parts of the voyage. Before the start of the race, Carlin's attitude was crystal clear. "For me, this race is going to be a quarter of a million dollar joy ride," he said. That's the one place where he was wrong. It cost him twice that, but he didn't seem dismayed. He's also credited with having said, "I am a full-time family man and a part-time sailor. When I decided to compete in this race, I vowed it would be for the fun of it." He had more than fun.

§

All seventeen of the competing yachts assembled at Vernon Shipyard in Portsmouth with still a million last-minute things to do. Everything had to be checked and counted. Food, radio equipment, rope, sails, cameras, and all other supplies were stashed away. The day before leaving was a madhouse jumble of reporters and photographers, riveting in for the best, last stories and pictures. Everyone was photographed at least a hundred times. But not Carlin. He had flown in two Mexican priests from Ireland and they had a quiet blessing ceremony for *Sayula II*. Champagne and Holy Water, both the right vintage. The night before leaving, everyone clung close to their boats and thoughts. Not Ramon Carlin, his family, or his crew. They were in a huge hotel suite nearby having a family fiesta. Mañana could wait 'til tomorrow; it was tequila time that night.

Chay Blyth had one of those Spartan statements ready for his departure. "All I need is a sailbag and a Union Jack." Further proof of his dead serious nature was his refusal of Whitbread's offer of unlimited quantities of their beer—an offer made to all participants to make the voyage easier. Blyth's men were stuck with that curry and water again, and don't think they didn't hate it. The only relief they got from it was when the water system on *Great Britain II* failed; they were foodless until repairs were made because the curry was dehydrated. The curry wasn't even for the birds. Peter Bates, one of Blyth's crewmen, swears that a small bird landed on the yacht, ate some of the curry, and promptly fell into the sea and drowned. As if it wasn't hard enough to get through meals on *Great Britain II*, Blyth threw all the cutlery—like civilized knives and forks and spoons—overboard in order to reduce unnecessary weight. Mary, Queen of Scots, had an easier life than Blyth's crew. It got worse. As the voyage progressed, *Great Britain II* lost three in crew. One of the men was swept overboard and drowned, another left the yacht in the first available port with a broken arm and no regrets, and a third got off at Capetown because he couldn't stand it any longer. Fine compatible bunch, Mr. Blyth.

To be fair to Blyth, as time went by he loosened up a little. At Capetown he took on ten cases Whitbread's ale, and in Sydney he took on twenty cases more. Is ale good with curry? Well, it's more compatible than water.

The quiet, unassuming and practically unknown Señor Ramon Carlin wound his merry way down the South Atlantic to Capetown. He wasn't having any crew problems at all. Two members of his crew had never laid eyes on him before they left Portsmouth, but he knew all about them. He knew a lot about everyone on his boat. *Sayula II* was like a mini-United Nations. Along with family members, Carlin had British, Dutch, Australian, and American crew members. If you had looked closely, you would have found that every single one of them was selected for his tough yachting skill and specialized knowledge.

On the second leg, from Capetown to Sydney, Carlin took on Yvonne Van der Byl as his navigator. She had left *Jakaranda*, a yacht that lasted for only the first leg of the race. *Sayula II* won the second leg with la Van der Byl at the helm. Suddenly, the Mexican yacht and Ramon Carlin became the cynosure of all eyes. Right into focus they came, and no one ever lost sight of them again.

The second leg of the race took the yachts from Capetown to Sydney, and the third leg from Sydney to Rio. Like Sir Francis Chichester before them, they had grim sailing through the Rip-Roaring Forties, so named because of the roaring winds below the fortieth parallel. Not one of the yachts got off lightly in the Forties. They battled sixty-mile-an-hour winds, mountainous waves, snow, and hail. *Sayula II* virtually capsized, rolling through 150 degrees, as she "fell off" a huge wave. Two of her crewmen were washed overboard but hauled themselves back with their harnesses. The yacht was awash below decks, wetting down supplies of chili and tamales, but otherwise not dampening too many spirits. *HMS Endurance* stood by when the yachts rounded Cape Horn. *Sayula II* was the second to do so, and *HMS Endurance* blasted forth with Mexican mariachi music. Ramon Carlin—the Cantinflas of the yachting world—and his crew and family danced the Mexican Hat Dance as they got around the Horn and headed for Rio.

Señora Carlin hated missing that party. She hadn't been aboard for the second leg, the most dangerous part of the voyage, but she was right there in Rio to greet them. And guess what was going on in Rio? That's right. Carnival. All the Carlins went to all the parties, and Daddy Carlin gave one too. As usual, a gay time was had by all. The possibility of winning had become a reality and the momentum was growing. The Carlin compatibility level was high. All the way around the world, *Sayula II* kept up a happy, carefree attitude. Enrique Carlin played a mean Mexican guitar every evening possible. If music hath charms, Enrique was sorely needed on *Great Britain II*. Blyth had achieved very little so far, for all his discipline.

By now, it was apparent that Ramon Carlin was about as casual about winning the 'round-the-world race as Space Control is in Houston when something goes wrong on a moon shot. Along with winning the race, Carlin should have won an Academy Award for Best Actor. While Blyth, an experienced sailor, was busy making the race the seven-month siege it was, Carlin was busy making it look easy. He threw up a smoke screen of gaiety that made his joy ride a winning race.

On Easter Sunday he blew back into Portsmouth, the winner and new champion. Handicapping is complicated in ocean racing. *Sayula II* was first for the Complete Race. She was second on the First Leg, first on the Second Leg, and second on the Third Leg. Chay Blyth beat *Sayula II* on only one leg, the fourth, when he ran second. By that time he had loosened up and gotten some decent food and beer in him, but it was too late.

No one knew much about Ramon Carlin going out. When *Sayula II* got back, everyone knew him. "His great secret was to know how to pick people and how to keep his ship happy," one of the newspapers rhapsodized. Isn't that what Chay Blyth had set up such a racket about seven months before?

Against all odds, in a standard boat, Ramon Carlin and his happy-go-lucky yachtsmen from the seven nations, collectively sailing under the Mexican flag, had beaten the best in the world. They worked hard. They played hard. And they won. The diminutive Ramon Carlin, family man and happy millionaire, was the biggest winner of them all.

11

Even the Lifeboats Had Lifeboats

The biggest and best private yacht in America, ever, was owned by a woman. The yacht was *Sea Cloud,* although that was not her name in the beginning. The woman was Marjorie Post, and that *was* her name in the beginning. She was heiress to a vast cereal fortune. She was almost excessively rich, she was lavishly beautiful, she was adventurous, and she had a flock of husbands.

She also had a flock of houses that made the White House seem like a nice little second home. Her camp in the Adirondack Mountains was on a private lake, reached by private motor boat and a funicular. Her home in Washington, D.C., had a bigger park than the one that surrounds Buckingham Palace. Her Palm Beach mansion faced both lake and sea, hence its name, Mar Lago. Since her death in 1974, finding someone to own and maintain her royal residences has not been easy. Some have been left to the government, but even the government can't seem to afford them. The style of living to which Marjorie was accustomed was way out of most people's leagues. She was one of those woman who have everything.

Except a yacht. Yachting was quite unknown to her until she married Edward F. Hutton, founder of the brokerage firm of E.F. Hutton & Company, and no mean millionaire himself. When he and Marjorie were married, he introduced her to yachting—in a big way. Although Marjorie was a late bloomer in yachting, Ed Hutton was not. He grew up with sailboats and progressed to sailing yachts, naming all of them *Hussar* and painting each one black. He loved the sea and sailing and yachts with a passion. The minute they were married, the Huttons started working on plans for a huge new yacht which would, of course, be called *Hussar* and would be painted black.

Marjorie took to the project like a duck to water. *Hussar* was two years in the building in Kiel, Germany, but her future mistress didn't let any grass grow under her feet waiting for it to be delivered. She planned the furnishings and trappings of *Hussar* right down to the tiniest detail. She rented a huge loft where everything was stored, awaiting delivery of the yacht, and she had a chalk plan drawn on the loft's concrete floor, indicating exactly where each piece of furniture was to be placed and listing where porcelains, linens, and silver were to be stored. When *Hussar* was delivered, presto! Everything was slipped into its rightful place without an ounce of confusion. The Huttons were ready to go.

And go they did. *Hussar* was no ordinary yacht, in any way. She was a four-masted bark, carrying thirty towering sails that were covered with 30,000 square feet of canvas. She cost $900,000 to build in 1931, and a quarter of a million dollars to maintain annually. She had a crew of seventy-two whose uniforms alone added up to some $20,000 a year. *Hussar* flew the American flag and she was the biggest, best, most beautiful and luxurious yacht in the whole wide world. A real dream boat.

Marjorie and Ed Hutton both adored *Hussar* from the moment they set foot on her, and so did their small daughter, Nedenia. Deenie, as she was nicknamed, is also known as actress Dina Merrill, and as Mrs. Cliff Robertson, wife of the Academy Award winning actor. She remembers all of her years aboard tenderly. After Christmas, instead of going back to school like other kids, Deenie, with her parents, would leave and pick up *Hussar*, usually in Florida, and go off for sometimes as long as six to seven months. Ed Hutton planned the long cruises to the Pacific, the South Atlantic, the Caribbean, or wherever they wanted the winds to take them.

"I grew up on *Hussar*," Deenie says. "Some wag once said that she was so huge that even the lifeboats had lifeboats, but she was home to me. One of the great things about Daddy was that when we set off on a long trip, he never made us keep to a precise schedule. If we liked it somewhere, we would stay until we'd had enough, and if we hated it, we'd beat it out of there right away. I never had any friends my own age because they were always in school. We would leave right after Christmas and would be gone for six or seven months. The crew were my friends. Most of them were Scandinavian-American. The captain's name was Lawson but he was Cappy to all of us. He made a perfect, painstaking model of the ship while she was being built so Mother and Daddy could see exactly how she was going to look. I have it now. I have so many of her things. In the main salon, which was done in fine English walnut furniture, there was a great Georgian desk that is in my apartment in New York now. All over the ship, there were a dozen or so of the most beautiful paintings of the sea off the Cornish coast, done by an Englishman, David James. Mother loved them and I loved them, and I have them, too. Whenever I look at them, I remember how it was then. Can you imagine what it was like to be aboard in a good spanking breeze, with the sails set and a full moon?

"Life was fairly simple on the long cruises. I'd do my schoolwork early with Mrs. Stylter, my governess-teacher, then I'd meet Daddy in the crew's galley and we would have a huge breakfast of eggs or pancakes and bacon and sausages and fresh bread from the ovens, all fattening things like that. Big Willie and Little Willie were the two chefs, and they stood over us like two great Prussian types if we didn't eat everything in sight. We had two doctors aboard, too, called Senior and Junior, but it was Mother who kept us healthy. She was passionate about exercise. She'd come up on deck in her royal blue leotard and we'd all do our exercise. Father would work with his punching bag and weights. Mother was as strong as she could be. She'd lie on her back and bounce me in the air on her feet as if we were clowns in a circus. When we were exhausted, one of the crew members would turn a firehose on us and that salt water was so cold and fresh that we'd all scream when it hit us, but it made us feel absolutely marvelous.

"Whenever we could, we'd swim in the open sea. We had a huge net that was strung from the bow, big enough so we could have a good swim together without worrying about sharks. We fished and we shot, and one day Daddy shot a flamingo. Mother wanted to have it mounted for the camp in the Adirondacks but Daddy couldn't skin it. Mother got a huge knife and sat cross-legged on the deck and did a quick, magnificent job of skinning it. 'Where in the world did you learn how to do *that?*' Daddy asked, incredulously. 'Hunting bears with my father in Alaska, dear,' she answered sweetly, as if she did that sort of thing every day."

§

For five years, the Huttons cruised all over the world. They were a welcome sight in every port of call. Sometimes guests would join them for a few weeks, but most often it was just the three of them. Plus a crew of seventy-two, that is. Marjorie was a natural diplomat. She gave huge dinners and receptions on *Hussar* whenever the occasion demanded, which was whenever she wanted to have a party. She entertained princes and paupers, but more often princes and heads of state and dictators and the like; they were a dime a dozen in those days.

Everyone wanted to be invited to *Hussar.* The most breathtaking view of her was with all her sails set, moving magnificently through the water. People who saw or knew her have never forgotten the sight of her under full sail, although her interiors were a knockout, too, and her creature comforts were extraordinary. The main salon and the dining room had Oriental rugs all over the floors. There was an exquisite marble, wood-burning fireplace with one of the David James seascapes above it. All furniture was fastened down with hooks and eyes to chain it to the floor. China and porcelain objects d'art were scattered around. Felt was glued to their bottoms, and the other side of the felt was then glued to the table or shelf they sat on so there could be no sliding or breaking. The mahogany dining table gleamed, mirrorlike, and had a two-inch frame that fit into it to prevent plates and cutlery from skittering down the table when the weather was rough.

Edward Hutton's private quarters were full of fine Early American furniture. His rugs were oval woven-rag rugs, and he had gathered a fine collection of scrimshaw, the carved shark teeth that sailors whittle away at to keep from going mad during long sea voyages. Marjorie's bedroom was painted a light pink, the drapes and bedspread were a pale, pale rose taffeta, and there was a pale Aubusson rug on her floor. The bathroom was pink marble with solid gold taps, that practical metal that never needs polishing. After all, a crew of seventy-two could hardly be expected to keep up with polishing a bunch of time-consuming bathroom fixtures. Deenie's quarters consisted of a bedroom and the sitting room where she did her lessons. Three double guest cabins, with a sitting room thrown in among them, were done in pale colors with soft-colored painted wooden furniture. One of the bedrooms was blue, one yellow, and all of the beds were canopied. *Hussar* was one smashingly gorgeous yacht.

"Memories flash back all the time like a kaleidoscope," Deenie recalls. "Sometimes I can't remember the year or which trip it was, but then a fragment will come back as clearly as if it happened yesterday. It seems as if we went to every fabulous and beautiful place in the world. Once we dropped anchor off Papeete and I remember seeing a young girl standing on the beach looking at us, holding her little boy's hand. She had a hibiscus in her hair. She watched us for a long time, and then the two of them came into the water and she swam out to us with the little boy's arms wrapped around her neck. We asked them aboard and gave them some ice cream and she looked at everything, smiling all the time. Then she thanked us very shyly and went down the ladder and, for some reason, I could never forget how she looked with the flower in her hair, swimming back to shore with that little boy clinging to her.

"On the greatest trip of all, we went to the Galapagos Islands, then down to Hawaii and the South Pacific, and back to California. In the Galapagos we adopted a huge land turtle that Mother named Jumbo. Zane Grey was with us that time, and he told us that Jumbo was possibly one hundred fifty years old. Father wanted his shell at first, but we all got so fond of him that he became the ship's pet, and he had the run of it. He would manage to get through the swinging doors into the main salon, and we'd come upon him wedged under a couch or under the desk. He adored Mother, and he adored lettuce. One afternoon we were having a reception on deck for about sixty big shots. Mother was waiting there for guests to arrive, wearing the most lovely pale green chiffon tea gown. Jumbo took one look at her and—chomp!—he went after her dress. His jaws closed down on the hem and they began a tug of war that Jumbo won because he tore the dress right off of her. We were all yelling and screaming and laughing at him, but nothing would make him let go. That was the end of her beautiful, lettucy dress. She fled below to change, and we put Jumbo away somewhere for that party. When we got to Hawaii, we found out we couldn't bring him back into America so we left him at the zoo in Honolulu. Just before we left, we went out to the zoo to say goodbye, and when Mother called 'Jumbo, Jumbo!' he came right out and she fed him a banana. We all wept because we had to leave him."

Deenie's childhood was good training for diplomacy. She was never a lonely child, but she did spend more than half her childhood in the company of grownups, living under somewhat extraordinary circumstances. Her father was

119

a quiet man who preferred exploring and sports and simple things, but he and Marjorie were aware that their yacht cut quite a figure and they delighted in inviting newcomers, including a king or two, aboard. Once, in Oslo, they invited King Haakon and Queen Maude to dine. Haakon was Deenie's first king. "He had on a *business* suit," she moaned. "I was so disappointed, I could have died. 'Where is your ermine robe and crown?' I asked, when they introduced us, but even though it was rude of me, he understood at once. 'Oh, my dear child,' he said, 'it was such a hot day that I left them at home.' "

§

Worlds and times change, and so they did for *Hussar*. The Huttons divorced. Good taste made a mystery of the reason. Why they parted was their business and remained so. All anyone knew was that Marjorie got custody of *Hussar*. Why? Had she fallen so in love with yachting that she was not about to give up her first child of the sea? Was Edward Hutton not able to maintain *Hussar*? Certainly his wife was much richer than almost anyone, but he too was a rich man and it was he, after all, who had been the longtime lover of yachting, long before he even met Marjorie. Did Marjorie take possession of the yacht to spite him, or to prove that she could take *Hussar* away whether he liked it or not? Did they fight over her?

Whatever the reasons, *Hussar* was Marjorie's property. Edward Hutton turned his back on yachting forever. He never built another yacht, he never set foot on one, and he never discussed it. There was a deep silent hurt that Deenie felt, even though she was still a child. "I'd come and tell him something wonderful that had happened on a trip and he would get a vague, faraway look in his eye. Or I'd want him to know about a crew member he was particularly fond of, but I soon realized he didn't want to hear anything at all. It was over for him. I was hurt, too, because we all loved her so, and she was such an unforgettable part of our lives. But there was a wall there and I could never get over it."

Marjorie had *Hussar's* black hull painted white as the breast of a gull and changed her name to *Sea Cloud.* "I know Mother wanted to change the identity and the look of the ship as much as she could. The past was the past," Deenie recalls. "As for me, I actually preferred her painted black, but I always loved the name *Sea Cloud,* and that's exactly what she looked like."

Sea Cloud was not the only one whose name changed. Marjorie married Joseph E. Davies, a Wisconsin lawyer who was a friend and advisor and a future ambassador. Marjorie obviously liked him, but Deenie was not his most ardent fan. "Joe Davies was very different. We didn't go on the great long trips I loved as a child, as we had with Father. Now the trips were shorter. Joe was more interested in the power play, and making hay with the diplomats and the big shots. Mother rather liked it all; it was a new scene for her and one that she was extremely good at. But it was never the same for me. Besides, Joe was no seaman. He was terrified of the sea; he knew nothing about it and he got seasick. What made me maddest of all happened on our way to Rio. We had planned a great celebration for King Neptune when we crossed the Equator, but we never got anywhere near the Equator. The sea got high and Joe ordered us back. We had never gone back before, but this time we turned around and fled. I was ready to kill Joe for that, but half the time he was ready to kill me too—as you can imagine, since I even went on their honeymoon trip with them."

The fact that Joe Davies didn't strangle his stepdaughter showed his diplomatic prowess. Once, when *Sea Cloud* lay at anchor in Dominican waters, the Davies gave an informal state dinner for Trujillo, then dictator of the Dominican Republic. It was the first time Trujillo saw *Sea Cloud,* but not the last. Joe Davies put Deenie in charge of dinner music—a fatal gesture, as it put her in a position to have at him for any real or imagined slights. From her post behind the curtain that hid the music machine from view, she was to play soothing dinner music, and also to watch for the end of the dinner. Then she was to put on the national anthem of the Dominican Republic, and that would give Joe the signal to propose the first toast. Deenie revved things up a bit by putting the record on at the end of the soup course. Joe looked slightly startled, but rose to and for the occasion, and proposed a most complimentary toast. Trujillo responded, and dinner progressed — until the end of the fish course, when Deenie obligingly put the record on again. Eight courses are the normal fare for an informal state dinner, and Deenie played the national anthem at the end of each one. Joe Davies, Trujillo, and the assembled guests rose, toasted, and accepted toasts at the end of each course. By the end of dinner, everyone was exhausted. Except Joe. He went after Deenie with murder in his eye. But to no avail, as Deenie says. "When he finally did catch me, I played innocent and pretended that I thought I had done exactly as he wanted me to do."

Distant thunder boarded *Sea Cloud* in the form of Ramfis Trujillo, although no one suspected it at the time. He and Deenie were around the same age so she, naturally, played hostess to the dictator's son. It was loathing at first sight. When Deenie asked Ramfis what he would like to drink, he said he thought some champagne might be nice. "Well, you can't have any," she told him. "We don't serve champagne to kids your age." The two of them were off and running. Ramfis settled for some grapes rather than what comes from them. He spat the seeds all over the deck, infuriating Deenie, who fought him into picking them up. That was only the beginning. "He was a rotten little kid," Deenie says, "but I was on to him, and I figured he'd try to find some way to pay me back. Dinner was to be late that night, so I was sent to bed and Ramfis was given one of the guest cabins. I had a hunch he'd try to come into my cabin to scare me. But with his sort of background, who knows what he had in mind. I kept my head hidden under the covers and waited, listening for him. When I heard the door open, very, very quietly, and heard him move towards me, I pretended I was asleep until he got right to the edge of my bed. Then I threw back the covers and screamed 'BOOO!' at the top of my lungs and jumped on him. He let out a screech like an animal, and tore out of my room yelling his head off. He went right up into the salon and threw himself at his father, weeping and wailing, and going on about how awful I was and he *made* his father take him off the ship right then and there. He was no favorite of mine, ever. And he got at me years later, many years after Mother had sold *Sea Cloud* to Trujillo. Ramfis brought her out to Los Angeles. I was working in a film at the time, and either as a courtesy or to upstage me—I'm not sure which—he invited me to come aboard. He had mounted a gun on her forepeak. That classified her as a warship, which meant they didn't have to pay dockage charges. He filled her up with every cheap starlet in Hollywood and I *hated* his being anywhere near my yacht, much less owning her and using her like that. When his father was assassinated, Ramfis filled her up with gold bars and tried to get out of the Dominican Republic. But they knew what he was up to, and they caught him and brought him back with all that gold he was trying to steal."

Gold touched *Sea Cloud* more than once long before she was sold to Trujillo. One late afternoon after a rain shower, a rainbow touched the deck. Marjorie was ecstatic. "One of us is going to get the gold," she said. "There's always a pot of gold at the end of the rainbow, you mark my words." Sure enough, Joe Davies' Irish valet had a sweepstakes ticket, and when they got home, they found he had won $100,000. He retired instantly, much to Joe's annoyance, but Marjorie never stopped reminding all of them about the rainbow.

Although *Sea Cloud*'s trips were shorter and more social now, she was still in constant use. When Joseph E. Davies was appointed ambassador to Russia in 1937, *Sea Cloud* went right along with them. She spent one summer moored in the harbor in Leningrad, and the Russians had a hard time coping with her. The comrades of Stalin's day knew nothing about the great Russian royal yacht, *Standart*, which had figured so prominently in the lives of the Czar and the Czarina before the revolution. The fact that *Sea Cloud*, the glorious four-masted sailing bark in their harbor, belonged to an individual was beyond them. Even the Intourist guides assigned to the Davies family were not allowed to board the yacht, for they would see firsthand how an American could live and, worse yet, they might even envy it. In Moscow, the Davies had Intourist guides glued to them, but in the port city of Leningrad, they sat on the quay and watched their quarry from afar.

Deenie spent that summer with her mother and stepfather. "One day, it was terribly hot. There was no wind at all and the harbor was full of smells, so we decided to go to a nearby island to have a swim and cool off. We had to take a pilot with us. The poor pilot who came aboard was dazzled out of his mind by the yacht. When we got to the island it was much cooler and cleaner, and we asked him if he would like to swim with us. It scared him to death. He told us that the island was Finnish and if he got anywhere near it, they would shoot him. While we swam, I looked up at the poor devil leaning against the rail in his hot uniform and I realized what a different world they lived in."

§

During World War II *Sea Cloud* did her service as proudly as any admiral. She was offered to and accepted by the Coast Guard. Her crew wanted to go with her, but no dice. Her masts were removed, her sails stored in Boston, and she went sub chasing in the North Atlantic. She came home loaded down with stripes and ribbons and chevrons, unscathed but bedraggled. Marjorie sent her to the shipyard in Jacksonville to be refitted. As Deenie tells it, "We went down to see her when she first got back and I wish we hadn't. We didn't expect her to look the same, anymore than a person does after a long war, but she really looked awful. Mother had to put her together again. It took some doing, but she was finally restored to her good old self."

§

Marjorie Post took great pride in the fact that *Sea Cloud* flew only the American flag. As it turned out, Marjorie was the great lady of American yachting. No other man or woman had owned a larger yacht based in American waters. Emily Cadwallader's *Savarona III* was larger, but never flew the American flag and was never closer to the United States than Bermuda. Marjorie loved *Sea Cloud* deeply, and she spent more than twenty years on her. After the war they cruised for several years as they had before, but the seamen's union had gotten too strong for even a woman of Marjorie's means to be able to afford *Sea Cloud* any longer. The monthly payroll alone was over $20,000, and never mind the total cost of maintaining the yacht. Marjorie wanted her crew to have new uniforms twice a year and that added another $20,000 to the budget. The days of luxury yachting had ended, even for *Sea Cloud*.

§

In 1954 Marjorie sold *Sea Cloud* to Trujillo for one million dollars. He'd had his eye on her for years and he wasn't faced with any seamen's union. He christened her *Angelita*. After his assassination in 1961, when his family made an unsuccessful attempt to escape on *Angelita*, the Dominican Republic sold her to a Louisiana businessman who converted her into what he hoped would be the greatest charter yacht of them all. He renamed her *Antarna*. He did a fine job refitting her, but it didn't work. *Antarna* is just sitting in Panama. But *Sea Cloud*, glorious *Sea Cloud*, is no more.

"She was so much a part of my life, and that part of my life is gone forever," Deenie says.

"I was in a car in Miami once, before she was sent to Panama, and I suddenly caught a glimpse of her over near the 33rd Street causeway. The driver found a way for us to get over there and I was so glad to see her, I just wanted to touch her and pat her and tell her how much I'd missed her.

"Even to this day, all it takes is a whiff of diesel oil to take me back. Whenever we pulled into a harbor, no matter what time of day or night it was, I'd hear the engines stop and reverse and I'd beat it lickety-split right up onto the bridge. I loved every moment of my life on *Sea Cloud* and I'll never forget it. Never."

12

Romance on the High Seas

Yes, Virginia, they do smoke pot and have orgies on yachts, thank heavens, although shipboard romances are a more legendary pursuit. You can't just hang around talking about navigation or how lousy the caviar is all the time, can you? When the moon is full and the music is playing, it all seems pretty romantic. A shipboard romance is like no other, aided and abetted as it is by luxurious but close surroundings.

A shipboard romance can develop into a triangle — sometimes with the ship being the third party. At least that's the way one might read the Jackie Kennedy and Aristotle Onassis story. Jackie was no stranger to luxury or power when she first met Onassis, but her introduction to Onassis proved to be her first taste of the fabulous world of yachting.

Jackie was the wife of the President of the United

States when her sister, Lee Radziwill, arranged for her to be invited for a cruise on *Christina*. Ari pulled out every stop to impress her, and he succeeded beyond his wildest dreams.

Ari was more impressed by Jackie than by any woman he'd ever met. It was probably her behavior in the face of tragedy that most impressed him. The Greeks are the great tragedians, and Ari's sympathetic instincts were heightened by the position that Jackie found herself in when the President was assassinated. Five years passed between the time of Jackie's first cruise on *Christina* and the day of her marriage to Onassis. During those years, every other woman in Ari's life faded into insignificance — except *Christina*. *Christina* was not only Ari's favorite material possession, but she turned out to be his most valuable possession when it came to the pursuit of Jackie. Let's face it. When Ari called, Jackie came running — to *Christina*.

The creamy white yacht played a major role in Jackie's life, far beyond the alliance formed between Jackie and Ari during that first meeting, when they got to know each other the way two people can get to know each other only on a yacht. From first to last, *Christina* figured in every major scene of the Kennedy-Onassis relationship. There were several more trips on the yacht and then, once Ari was sure of winning Jackie, his courtship took a brief turn toward negotiating the financial end of their romance. After all, flesh is peddled on yachts in more ways than one. The thought of the cool Jacqueline Kennedy sipping tea on the deck of *Christina* while she and Aristotle Onassis discussed the details that eventually evolved into fourteen pages of premarital agreement seems quite logical. Considering *Christina*'s role in the romance, what better place to work it all out?

Christina was in on the honeymoon, too. Eleven days after they were married, they went off on a honeymoon cruise that had been delayed because of some big business deal of Ari's. The romance with *Christina* didn't end with the honeymoon. They had hardly gotten ashore before they were back aboard again. Jackie and Ari spent their first Christmas together on a cruise, accompanied by the Kennedy children. During their marriage Jackie often flew to join Ari and *Christina*, no matter where they were. Once, she arrived in the Canary Islands, boarded *Christina* to join Ari, and the two of them were alone for nine days en route to Trinidad, seeing no one but each other and an occasional crew member. *Christina* was the site Ari chose to shower Jackie with a king's ransom in jewels. For her first birthday party as Madame Onassis, he turned up with some rubies that still bring forth gasps when mentioned by even the most sophisticated among us. *Christina* was always there for them, even at the end. When Ari died in Paris, Jackie brought his body home to Greece and put him aboard his beloved *Christina* for his last voyage, to his burial place on the island of Skorpios.

§

As world shattering as the Kennedy-Onassis pairing was, it had nowhere near the impact of another romance that came to a head on a yacht many years before. In 1938 Edward VIII was the uncrowned king of England. The woman he loved, the twice-married Wallis Simpson, had now been twice divorced. The world was watching every move the famous lovers made and England was in an uproar, even though all reports of the "unsuitable" romance had been effectively throttled in the British press.

Edward, the uneasy and spoiled king, desperately wanted to get away from all the hullabaloo. What better way for a man in love than on a yacht? The royal yacht, *Victoria and Albert*, wasn't suitable under these circumstances and, unlike Onassis, he had no *Christina* on which to set sail into the blue. The king turned to his old friend, Lady Yule, who graciously chartered her yacht, *Nahlin*, to him. Lady Yule generally traveled for months on end on *Nahlin*, and to get some exercise every day she had equipped the yacht with a gymnasium that had enough gadgets to keep the entire British army in shape. Heaven knows if the king and his lady from Baltimore ever used it, but it was available to them.

One thing is for sure: Wallis Simpson had allure for

more than one head of state. *Nahlin's* cruise took them to Istanbul, where Ataturk, the dictator of Turkey, took a fancy to her. The Turkish government had recently bestowed Emily Cadwallader's huge *Savarona* on their adored dictator, and he arranged a dinner party on *Savarona* in honor of Edward VIII and his party. When the king and his aides arrived without Mrs. Simpson, Ataturk demanded to know where she was. Fruity Metcalf, an *aide-de-camp* to the king, explained that they had thought only gentlemen were expected. "Ridiculous," said Ataturk. "We dine only after Mrs. Simpson has arrived." Which she did, very shortly afterwards.

Nahlin's long-dallying cruise through the Aegean Sea and along the Dalmatian coast of Yugoslavia had everything to do with the little gold band that Edward eventually put on Wallis's eager finger. He had already made up his mind that he would have what he wanted, but the yacht trip sealed his fate. There they were, in perfect luxury and privacy, surrounded by a few dear and trusted friends on a dream of a yacht. What more could they want?

At the end of the cruise, the man who could have been king had he wanted to, decided he wanted Wallis Simpson more. They would marry. They probably never would have arrived at that decision had they been on a hiking trip in the Black Forest. Oh, there is nothing like a yacht.

§

There is also nothing quite as maddening as a nosy, frustrated hostess who has to know who is sleeping with whom on her yacht. One overly curious lady used to sprinkle cornmeal in the halls outside of her guest cabins. Telltale footprints in the morning light told every story — until one of her more experienced night-roaming romantics bought his very own box of cornmeal to cover his tracks. The gentleman was her husband and the owner of the yacht.

§

Adnan Khashoggi wouldn't give a hoot if the cornmeal were waist high. Khashoggi is a Saudi-Arabian multi-millionaire who made his fortune by importing automobiles, air conditioners, and refrigerators into his native land. He is the swingingest Arab of them all, and the thought of no sex or romance or hugging or kissing while yachting is totally repugnant to the sailing Saudi.

All men like girls — well, nearly all — but the nice thing about Khashoggi is that he loves yachts too. Most rich oil men from the Middle East don't share his zest. They might charter for a week, but they rarely own yachts. Adnan does. He owns three nice big yachts, and one of them is a 145-foot lady called *Khalidia*. If you judged by the size of the guest list — Khashoggi always seems to have at least forty people staying on board — you'd think *Khalidia* was twice that size. When there gets to be too much of an overflow, which often happens, Adnan simply calls for one of his other yachts to handle the traffic.

Khashoggi has wives, children, and girl friends in grandiose numbers. In his private collection alone, there are five concubines. They are never far from his sight and they are accompanied by five children of undetermined origin plus two British nannies. *None* of the concubines are good Arab girls. There's a gorgeous Brazilian, a striking Argentine, a chic French girl who has never been seen in anything more or less than a bikini (except by Adnan), a typical English rose of a girl, and a warm Italian signorina. Variety is the spice of master Khashoggi's yachting life. Well, what else are girls and yachts for?

§

Variety is fine, but things can get too spicy if you're not careful when it comes to selecting your romantic partners. April Ashley, a tall, gorgeously proportioned English personality, came knocking on the side of *Shemara* when she pulled into the quay in Ibiza one summer. When Serge Semenenko was told who his deep-voiced guest was, he suggested that they might meet after dinner in one of the popular local bistros. When Serge and his party had finished dinner and were about to depart, he found that his captain, who had joined them for dinner, had disappeared.

They found him sitting at the bar with April Ashley. He was already a little bit drunk, and the alluring Miss Ashley was persuading him to have another brandy. The captain had taken a mad fancy to April and was stroking her arms and shoulders, muttering about what beautiful breasts and skin she had. It was difficult to drag him away, but the group succeeded in getting him back aboard and out of April's clutches. It wasn't until days later that Serge took it upon himself to explain to the good captain that April had been George until a short time before "she" had happened upon the captain. The captain hasn't looked at a woman since. That experience was enough to cure any yachter of romantic inclinations.

§

Rex Harrison should know a woman when he sees one. Or hears one. But even "sexy Rexy" was once taken in by a case of mistaken identity.

He had chartered Loel Guinness's *Calisto* for a month and was at dockside in Calvi, one of the most spectacular ports in Corsica. Some English friends had joined Rex, who was then married to British actress Rachel Roberts. After dinner on board, Rex retired and Rachel and her guests went ashore to the local bistro for some music and a nightcap. Hours later, they returned to the yacht, all drunker than sailors, which is as it should be. Rachel Roberts has collected stray animals, particularly cats, from one end of the earth to the other. The cat she found strolling the port in Calvi had obviously been waiting for her to save him. She picked him up and stroked him and assured him that she would take care of him for life.

When Rachel and her friends returned to the yacht, everyone made some attempt to be quiet in order not to disturb the sleeping Rex. Rachel tiptoed down the hall to the master cabin, cat in arms, and cautiously opened and closed the cabin door, shushing the cat all the while. Once inside the cabin, the cat let out a screaming yowl that would have raised the dead. Rachel almost jumped out of her skin. Not Rex. Coming to from the depths of his sleep, he sweetly inquired, "Is that you, Rachel?"

§

Actors love yachts, sometimes simply because they can get away from the public eye, and sometimes because they want to play games that they might not indulge in on dry land.

The calm of one Sunday morning was shattered for the crew and anyone else within earshot by the appearance on deck of a sensational-looking girl who was wearing nothing more than a bath towel and a recognizable perfume. She came up on deck, screaming like a banshee. "You'll not f_____ me again, you bastard," she screeched looking to the cabin below—and then jumped overboard.

"Let the double-crossing bitch drown," roared the naked man who careened right up onto the deck after the girl. It was hardly a romantic statement.

The girl was howling her head off. She'd forgotten that she didn't know how to swim. The crew of the black schooner wasn't sure which of their impulses to follow. The girl had to be saved, but here was their boss bellowing at them to let her drown. Common sense prevailed. A launch was hurriedly put over the side and a drenched, bedraggled girl was brought back on board. All was forgiven, and the battling lovebirds disappeared below.

What were the names involved in this love story? The man was the romantic Errol Flynn. The girl's name is lost in playgirl history. The yacht was *Zaca*. The perfume was Joy.

§

Affairs are fine for those who prefer them, but there is something infinitely charming about the idea of honeymooning on a yacht. A lot of people have done it, but none so well as a sophisticated adventurer named Ben Finney. Ben never had much money but he had a best friend called Billy Leeds, heir to a tin fortune, who really was a best friend.

Ben, having romanced every girl he could get his mitts on, finally fell in love. Head over heels. On bended knee, he begged his beautiful redheaded Muriel to marry him. Knowing his track record, she took some time to think it over. Finally, she accepted.

As a wedding present, Billy and Olive Leeds took the Finneys around the world on their yacht, *Moana II*, which was a huge, converted Swedish freighter. She had a swimming pool, a platform for clay pigeon shooting, a doctor, a registered nurse, and a crew of fifty-four. What more could honeymooners need?

The Leeds and the Finneys left Miami within one hour after the ceremony and headed for the Panama Canal and the South Pacific. One year later, to the day, they returned to the 79th Street Yacht Basin in New York. A lonely figure was standing on the dock waiting for them. When the lines were tied up and the gangplank came down, Ernest Hemingway strolled casually aboard and said to Mr. and Mrs. Finney and Mr. and Mrs. Leeds, "Been away?"

§

Maybe it's not always dramatic, but sex does seem sexier and romance is more romantic on a yacht. It's all a dream world, and it's nice to know that it's more expensive to be bedded down on a yacht than it is in a suite at the Plaza.

And it's very soothing to be out of sight of prying eyes, far away from it all in your own private world. The crew knows what's going on, but they're not blabbermouths and it's part of yachting snobbery to keep your mouth shut about what's going on aboard *your* yacht. Oh, they may talk *next* summer, but this year they'll keep your affairs quiet. Ah, romance on the high seas! There's nothing quite like it.

13
Chickens of the Sea

Yachts are such beautiful toys. Yachting is such a lovely way to go from here to there, and yachters, as any fool can plainly see, are all rich and gorgeous and lead such glamorous lives. No wonder we would all like to have our own yacht. Yachting is a dream, in a dream world of calm seas, bright sun, and timeless pleasures. But it can easily become a nightmare.

It's no fun to go around worrying about the bad side of a beautiful world, but fear and foul play *are* a part of it and yachting can sometimes be a very scary business. Yachts have burned. They have piled up on rocks. They have collided with each other, shearing off a bow here, digging a hole in a hull there. Yachts have been slapped down by waves as high as 150 feet — "falling," as it is called — into sea trenches that break or capsize them. Others have sunk without a trace, disappearing forever. Yachts have been stolen right out from under an owner's nose, never to be seen or heard from again. Hair-raising things happen a lot of the time, including hijacking—or yacht-jacking, if you prefer. And thereby hangs a tale.

§

One night a few years ago, E.L. Doheny, a multimillionaire Californian, was lucky enough to be safely at home in his own bed at his own house in Honolulu. He was luckier than the crew of his 75-foot ketch, *Kamalii*, which sat in her slip at the Ala Wai Yacht Harbor. She had competed in the Trans-Pacific race from Los Angeles to Honolulu a few weeks before and was waiting for Larry Doheny to decide when he wanted to sail home to California. Her crew went ashore that evening to blow part of their paychecks and to finish provisioning *Kamalii* for her return trip. *Kamilii*'s crew consisted of Captain Bob Waschkeit, first mate Frank Power, and John Freitas, cook and able-bodied seaman. The three men were back aboard and sound asleep by eleven P.M.

Suddenly, Frank Power was awake. Someone had come aboard, just over his head, and was walking around. Several someones. Frank, still groggy with sleep, stumbled up to the bridge and ran head-on into a blinding flashlight and the unmistakable knowledge that the metal object being poked into his stomach was a pistol. When the light was turned out, he was faced with three men, two of them with knives in their hands. Right behind were his two shipmates. They had heard the noise, too.

Five minutes later *Kamalii*'s crew had been handcuffed, bound, gagged, and slung onto the floor of the main salon. The invaders brought duffel bags and rolls of charts aboard and then, again at gunpoint, dragged Captain Bob to the engine room and made him explain how to operate *Kamalii*.

It was only a matter of moments before *Kamalii* was backing out of her slip, making for the open sea. Captain Bob and his two mates were ungagged and then tied into berths in the master cabin, ankles and wrists still bound. No one at Ala Wai Yacht Harbor would pay any attention to *Kamalii's* departure; she had been expected to leave anytime. Larry Doheny could easily have boarded his yacht at midnight and taken off. Now, until he appeared and asked where the devil his yacht was, no one would even notice that she was missing. That could be days from now.

Kamalii's crew was pretty sure what was going to happen to them. The three men who had stolen the half-million-dollar yacht certainly intended to kill them. They would have to get rid of their only witnesses.

The three young men who had yacht-jacked *Kamalii* wore crew cuts. The one who seemed to be the leader was a former Coastguardsman, and the other two had been Marines and had served together in Vietnam. Just three clean-cut American boys. *Kamalii's* crew learned from their conversation that their captors planned to head for a small island they had found on their charts, that lay in a little-known area of the Pacific. Here, they would sink the yacht and establish a "groovy" commune, with peace and quiet for all. The three veterans, all in their early twenties, had lived in communes together in California and Hawaii. They had planned this little caper carefully. *Kamalii* suited them perfectly.

Captain Bob, Frank, and John were stripped of everything they owned; clothing, passports, watches, all identification, plus all of *Kamalii's* charts went overboard. At three the next afternoon, the yacht-jackers unbound *Kamalii's* helpless crew.

"Jump!" said their leader. The three peace-seeking yacht-jackers were going to force *Kamalii's* naked crew to jump into the ocean in shark-infested waters, 150 miles southwest of Hawaii and deep in the least traveled sea-lanes of all of the vast Pacific. Charming bunch of fellows to go sailing with, eh?

Captain Bob Waschkeit pled for their lives. He begged his captors for a life raft. The leader finally agreed to give them life jackets and made a half promise that he'd throw in a life raft once they were in the water. It was a more generous concession than expected, but Captain Bob was sure that the three buddies meant to get them in the water in their life jackets and then shoot them like sitting ducks. Life was looking about as grim as it could look. Having nothing else to do, the three men put on their life jackets.

"Jump," said the leader again. *Kamalii*'s men, heads down, stood firm. "Okay," said the young man. "We'll shoot you now and then shove you over."

Bob Waschkeit, Frank Power, and John Freitas looked at each other. Captain Bob shrugged his shoulders, and over they went. They quickly formed a triangle in the water, holding hands and watching as *Kamalii* sailed away. There was nothing they could do or say. They might have been better off if they had been shot.

Suddenly, *Kamalii* turned. Back she came. A rubber life raft was thrown into the sea beside them.

"You got lucky!" a voice shouted. "We tossed a dime and it came up life raft for you. You might as well have the dime, too." He tossed the small silver coin into the life raft, and then *Kamalii* was gone, this time for good. They were alone now, with only eight pints of water and four flares as provisions.

Fate looked kindly on the three crewmen. Five hours after they had been forced to jump into the sea and then been reprieved with a life raft, Frank Power saw a green light on the horizon. One of the flares was sent up instantly, and a second one a few minutes later. The freighter *Benadir* saw the flares and came to the rescue.

Benadir's engines had broken down twice and she was 1,300 miles off her course, far from any regular sea-lanes. Her Italian crew had taken weeks to make repairs. Meanwhile, they had drifted. As soon as they brought *Kamalii*'s crew on board, they fitted them out with clothing, overfed them with pasta, and radioed Larry Doheny and the Coast Guard in Honolulu to tell them what had happened. *Benadir* was heading for Yokohama and would arrive there in nine days' time.

On arrival in Yokohama, *Kamalii*'s men found that Larry Doheny had new passports and homebound tickets for them. Coast Guard aircraft had sighted *Kamalii* on an air-sea search the day after *Benadir's* message had been received in Honolulu. Two Coast Guard cutters intercepted *Kamalii* the next day. The yacht-jackers were in custody and *Kamalii* was on her way back to Hawaii. All's well that ends well.

Kamalii's crew weren't the only lucky ones in this story. The three yacht-jackers were imprisoned in Honolulu on charges of armed robbery, grand theft, kidnapping, and attempted murder — but the law is a law unto itself. For all this, they were sentenced to prison terms of two and a half years for the leader and two years each for the other two. Fourteen months later they were all free. They've probably gone off somewhere, seeking again some mythical "groovy" island where they can find some peace and quiet.

§

If the U.S. law ever catches up with Robert Vesco, he may find himself facing more charges than the yacht-jackers did. The fugitive financier has a 54-foot aluminum yacht named *Joya Poca*, which means "little joy." Very little, from all reports. Vesco is prepared to take on the entire U.S. Government, the Air Force, the Army, the Navy, the Marines, and anyone else who comes at him. Vesco's captain, Jay Cook (don't you love captains named Cook?), resigned from Mr. Vesco's employ and went to a Senate investigating committee with information that would shiver anyone's timbers.

Captain Cook reported he quit his job on *Joya Poca* because Vesco was equipping the ship with missiles. *Missiles* on a 54-foot yacht? Oh, yes. He said that she was also equipped with machine guns, rifles, pistols, and a wardroom full of ammunition, and that fifteen of Vesco's thirty bodyguards were armed to the teeth.

No one has shot at anyone yet. Vesco continues living in Costa Rica, ready to take off in his gunboat on split-second notice. The thought of a swift white yacht bristling with missiles and other such lethal weapons instead of lazy-ing about in the sun makes you wish Mr. Vesco had bought himself a battleship, doesn't it?

§

Just as it would be wise to steer clear of Mr. Vesco and his missiles, it might also be a good idea to stay away from the Bermuda Triangle. The Triangle stretches south from the Sargasso Sea, making a north point in Bermuda, a west point in Miami, and a south point in Puerto Rico. Over a thousand vessels have disappeared in the Triangle, and while many yachters feel it's all an out-of-control legend, there are just as many who avoid the area like the plague. Whatever the truth is, three best sellers have been written about the Triangle, and yet new tales keep surfacing all the time.

Phil and Chris Borden, two young California brothers, can make a believer out of you pretty quickly, if you can coax them to talk about the Triangle at all. Their parents were divorced many years ago. When their mother remarried, she married an experienced and devoted yachtsman, and for their honeymoon they sailed alone together from New York to Bermuda. Somewhere in the Triangle, they vanished.

Not a word was ever heard from them, not a trace ever found. Seven years later, in accordance with California law, Phil Borden, being the eldest son, went to court to declare his mother legally dead. "It was an eerie feeling to stand before a judge, in a court of law, and wonder for the ten thousandth time, what happened? Where did they go? What became of my mother?"

§

So it's not all glamour and smooth sailing, what with yacht-jackers, and armed, fugitive millionaires, and inexplicable disappearances. It must be especially terrifying to know that your yacht is sinking beneath you. Granted, it's a sober and scary business, but there's often a touch of the ridiculous, too. Some people save the silliest things when the ship is going down. Mike Powers, a strong and handsome and sensible young American, may have hit a new high, and his mother, Kelly, ran him a close second.

Mike's father, Bob, was the proud possessor of a converted PT boat named *Sable*. The Powers family cruised the Med every summer. In August they were in Greece. That's when the *meltemi*, or "bad time," comes, and the Aegean acts like the really rotten sea that it can be, for days on end. Howling winds, drenching rains, and high, rough seas can drive you mad. Where is all that blue and white beauty and bright sun that you came for?

Sable had lain by a small island for days, waiting for the weather to change. The weather remained beastly. Bad weather tries the patience of even the most experienced yachtsman, and just when they should lay low — and they know it — they opt for action. It is almost invariably a mistake. Bob Powers said, "Let's get out of this." His captain agreed, and they decided to cross to the mainland that night since the wind and sea are normally calm in the late evening. Not that night.

After two harrowing hours of plowing through angry seas, a huge wave hit *Sable* and slammed her onto a reef. She began to break up on the rocks, and she was floundering fast. The Powers, plus captain and crew, were taking to the lifeboats when Kelly Powers, Mike's beautiful mother, screamed, "No, no, I'm not going without my hair." As a child she had gorgeous red hair, long enough to sit on. When it was cut off, her mother saved the long hank for Kelly, who took great pride in her beautiful hairpiece. To lose it after all these years would be unthinkable. One of the sailors was dispatched to the master cabin, told what drawer the hair was in, and told to hurry — an unnecessary precaution under the circumstances. He raced off, found the hairpiece, returned and put it into his grateful mistress's hand. At that moment, a gust of wind hit them, and Kelly could no more have held on to her hairpiece than she could have swum to Athens. As she grabbed the sides of the lifeboat, all she could see was her red hair vanishing into the winds above the angry Aegean.

At least Kelly's choice was a sentimental one. Can

you possibly imagine what Mike Powers saved? His watermelon. He had ferreted out the only watermelon in Greece and he wasn't getting into any lifeboat without it. Back he went to his cabin, grabbed his beloved watermelon and returned to the lifeboat.

Bob Powers only wanted to save his yacht. When that was not possible, he was grateful that the reef they had struck was close to a small island where they could take shelter. The good Greek islanders took them in. The next morning, Mike shared his watermelon with one and all. And the Powers lived to tell the tale.

§

Christina certainly was a big, safe yacht, but one good storm can change a feeling of security into terror. One summer, Jackie and Ari Onassis were caught in the same sort of *meltemi* weather that the Powers had experienced. *Christina* took a blow from a mammoth wave that keeled her over hard. She seemed to take forever righting herself, wallowing as she did so. Jackie and Ari had separate sleeping quarters—not far from each other, you understand, but separate. When *Christina* rolled over, Jackie flew to Ari's side and jumped into bed with him like a frightened child. From then on, fair weather or foul, they shared the same bed. Who wants to sleep alone anyway, especially when the sea is raging? Now that Onassis is gone, neither Christina Andreadis, who owns three quarters of the yacht, nor Jacqueline Onassis, who owns the rest, has shown much inclination to take long cruises. Maybe they miss Ari, but they don't seem to miss the sea.

§

You'd think that seasickness would discourage would-be yachters as effectively as a healthy fear of the sea does, but t'ain't necessarily so. Yacht owners have been known to turn green setting foot aboard their favorite status symbol, but as long as status means more to them than seasickness, they'll battle it. The poor devils deserve sympathy, not ridicule. You own a $10 million yacht and you get seasick reading *Yachting* magazine in the doctor's office? How embarrassing. That *mal de mer* often comes from a deep-rooted, subconscious fear of the sea, and nothing annoys a rich man as much as being scared to death of the one possession he prizes above all others.

Armand Hammer, a tycoon and business genius, provides a reverse twist to the psychology of fear. Long before the jet airplane changed our lives, Armand made the crossing to Europe on business on one of the big liners several times a year. The minute he got aboard, he would go to his cabin, put on his pajamas, get into bed, and stay there for the entire trip, moaning and eating nothing. He would sip a little champagne from time to time, but he could hardly stand up and he hated every moment of every trip.

When he made his first *big* money in the whiskey distilling business, a friend said to him, "Armand, you must have a yacht now." Armand's eyes lit up. Of course he must have a yacht. The memory of all those ghastly crossings of the past didn't faze him at all. Naturally, he would organize and operate his *own* yacht better than anyone had ever done it before — and Armand Hammer is a man who really knows how to run his own show.

So he got a yacht. He was never, for one second, ever seasick again. A small postscript should be added. Armand Hammer has had three beautiful wives. The only picture he carries in his wallet is of his yacht.

§

Not everyone is cured of a fear of the sea simply by acquiring a personal yacht, but Malcolm Forbes (of *Forbes* magazine fame) found a way to beat the rap. He was determined to have his yacht and eat on it, too.

Forbes knew that he was terrified of the prospect of an ocean voyage but that he wasn't at all frightened as long as he was in full sight of dear old terra firma. That made everything peachy. He kept his hundred-foot *Highlander* at the 79th Street Yacht Basin and used her to commute.

Now, Vincent Astor used *Nourmahal* and J.P. Morgan used *Corsair* to commute from dirty old Wall Street out to their Long Island or Hudson River mansions in perfect luxury—in fact, that was part of the reason they built their yachts—but Forbes went them one better. He used *Highlander* to commute up the river to football games at West Point, a wildly expensive way to travel, especially during the Sixties, and he was cool as a cucumber—as long as he could see the river banks on either side.

Wintering in Florida and the Caribbean posed a slightly different problem for him, but not for long. *Highlander* took the inland waterway to Florida, which was even cosier than the Hudson route. On arrival in Palm Beach or Miami, he lived luxuriously on board his yacht and when the time came to move on to Nassau and Jamaica, *Highlander* sailed and Forbes flew.

Forbes adored his yacht. In fact, he used it more often than most owners, although the only explanation he ever offered was on behalf of his valet. "It's marvelous to have the yacht—none of that dreary packing and unpacking that my valet hates so." Oh, la!

§

The beautiful Frances Newman is another one who was scared to death of being out of sight of dry land, but she didn't mention it to her prospective husband, Augustus J. Newman, until she had that little gold band securely on her finger. Gus Newman adores yachting, and when he married Frances it never occurred to him that they wouldn't spend several months of each year sailing off into the sunset together.

Frances was not only beautiful, she was also very persuasive, and she prevailed upon Gus to hug the coastline wherever they went. Being a real sailor—and a smart one—Gus found a way to compromise. He plugged up all the portholes on his *Southern Breeze*.

Southern Breeze was 168 feet long, so Gus had a lot of porthole-plugging to do. But he did it and, as a result, you couldn't see out unless you went out. As long as she stayed inside, Frances could pretend that Cap d'Antibes was just off the bow. Believe it or not, it worked.

§

Canadian oil tycoon Frank McMahon had no need for portholes, plugged or unplugged, when he bought *Wildcatter.*

Frank and his wife Betty decided to get a divorce and then got into one of those family spats about who gets what. She wanted the Queen Anne and he wanted the Chippendale — you know how it is — so Frank took care of it all by taking it all. He bought *Wildcatter,* 127 feet of storage space, for a cool million dollars. When the van arrived at the McMahon mansion in Vancouver — whoosh! — everything went into storage on *Wildcatter.* Including Betty's clothes and books and files.

Frank's million-dollar storehouse then went off for cold storage in Alaska or Antarctica or some such exotic place. That's a successful way to play; tricky, but effective.

§

Man's imagination knows no bounds when it comes to figuring out new ways to cheat his fellow man. A young English couple who chartered the same small sailing yacht every year had an intriguing experience one summer in Sicily. They would pick up the boat in Naples and spend two or three weeks cruising in Italian waters. He was the captain and she was the crew.

One evening they were heading into Taormina when the girl noticed that they were running alongside a huge fishing net. She called to her husband at the tiller and said, "Look out! There's the biggest fishing net I've ever seen on our starboard side." Her husband looked and replied, "Not only that, but it's getting dark and that guy should have his running lights on." They pulled alongside the fishing boat and hailed the fisherman in Italian, telling him to show some light since he was dragging such a big net. The boatman started shouting at them, shaking his fists and gesturing as only an Italian can, threatening them with every possible misfortune if they didn't get away from him, and fast. The young couple was nonplussed by his ferocity. All that to-do about what? They sailed on, laughing. They put into Taormina and went up to a friend's villa for a dinner party. The girl found herself seated next to a formidable looking Sicilian, and she told him about the bad-tempered fisherman with the huge net.

"That wasn't a fishing net, my dear," her new companion said. "That was a yacht net."

"What do you mean, a yacht net?" she asked.

"That net catches yachts," he explained to her. "The man isn't a fisherman, either. He takes the boat out in the late afternoon and stays out most of the night. When he comes upon a good big yacht, he gets as close to it as he can and tries to get the propeller caught in his net. Then he sets up a howl the likes of which you heard today. He was only raising hell with you because you were of no interest to him and he wanted you out of his way, particularly at that time of day when the bigger yachts are making for port.

"The yachts he catches are in trouble. They've torn his net, they are cheating a poor fisherman out of the only way he can make an honest living—and he's going to see to it that they pay for it. They make for the nearest little port to disentangle and to settle up. On arrival, the local police, who are in on the plot, impound the yacht. Not only is the yacht owner stuck with paying for the net, he is also overcharged for berthing space, port taxes, and a lot of additional compensation for the police and the poor fisherman, who can't make his honest living again until his net has been repaired."

"My goodness," the girl said. "I'm glad we were of so little interest to the rotten son-of-a-gun. But how do you know so much about it? Has he caught you?"

"No, never," beamed the godfather-like Sicilian. "You see, I own the net."

14

A Tale of Two Sales

Selling a yacht can break your heart. You may be selling hundreds of happy hours of your life and doing away with your passport to freedom and your symbol of power.

Then again, selling a yacht can also make your day. That monstrous old tub had busted you with hidden costs you never dreamed of when you bought her. You've been cheated in every port in every country you touched, and even in some you didn't. Your captain has been solidly drunk for three years, and on *your* booze. You now remember the strange little smile on the face of the man you were sucker enough to buy the yacht from. It's the same smile you have on your face now as you contemplate the man who wants to buy from you. You remember how beautiful the yacht had seemed when you first saw her lying there, shimmering in the water. She was yours, all yours. Oh boy, *was* she!

So you've decided to sell? Fine. But no matter what your reasons, you're still not done with this yacht. You have one more story to tell about her, the tale of the sale, and it could be the worst or the best of the lot.

§

After three glorious years of cruising on *La Belle Simone*, covering more than 57,000 nautical miles, Bill Levitt decided to sell his "floating Taj Mahal," as he often referred to her. Everyone wanted to know why. There is no way a man can build, sail, and then sell a yacht like *La Belle Simone* — all within three years' time — without the rumors flying, especially a yacht that has garnered as much publicity as she had. Was Bill going broke? Was his marriage going sour? Was there something wrong with the yacht? The answer to all three questions was "No," much to the disappointment of the scandal sheets and even of some of the Levitt's jealous "friends."

Bill Levitt made a tough but wise decision. Owning a yacht as huge as *La Belle Simone* meant having one of the world's biggest and best white elephants on his hands. The energy crisis had tripled the price of fuel in one year and doubled the difficulty of getting it. Problems in the world of mini-wars — Greece, Turkey, Cyprus, Beirut, Israel, Egypt — had forced cancellation of some elaborately planned trips that Bill wanted to take. There were inevitable crew problems that always exist on a big yacht, although Bill had a minimum of trouble there: His crew respected him and were super loyal to him. They nicknamed him "the adorable tycoon."

"I want a yacht that I own, not a yacht that owns me. And I do not intend to run a hotel in the future as I have for the past three years," Bill Levitt said. So *La Belle* went on the block and Bill went back to the old drawing board. He had decided two things. His next yacht would be not more than 150 feet long, and he was keeping Klaus Gotsch, his captain of many years. It wasn't the first time that Bill had changed yachts and kept his captain. When he sold his first yacht, *Les Amis*, everything went — whether it was latched down or not—except Klaus Gotsch. A good captain is impossible to replace. Bill wasn't about to dispense with yachting or with Klaus Gotsch. He was simply shuffling the cards again and dealing from a new deck.

The asking price for *La Belle Simone* brought gasps. Sixteen million dollars. *Sixteen million dollars!* Was the bloody boat made of uranium? Everyone who had read the reams of publicity about her knew that she had cost "only" $8 million to build. Had good old Bill gone bonkers? No, he had not gone bonkers. And he immediately turned down an offer of $14 million, giving cause for more gasping. He *meant* sixteen mil, but that's not as crazy as it sounds. First of all, yachts are not like cars. A well-built, well-kept yacht increases in value. Ask any yacht broker, but don't believe him. Get an engineer and a naval architect to go over anything that you are thinking of buying that is bigger than a rowboat. Have patience when you buy and when you sell. Bill may regret not accepting that $14 million offer, but maybe not. As with everything else in life, timing is everything.

Today's escalating prices will make Bill's new yacht more expensive to build, but they also justify the asking price for *La Belle Simone*. A yacht the size of *La Belle* would cost much more than $16 million to build now, and that handful of greedy Greeks and Arabs who have their eyes on *La Belle* are aware of it. So is Bill Levitt. But Levitt is a good poker player. The asking price of *La Belle Simone* is more apt to go up than down, and he is more apt to get it than not. No matter how long it takes to sell her, just think of it this way. Lying in her winter home at Palma de Majorca—fallow, untenanted and with a skeleton crew—*La Belle Simone* costs less than half of what it would cost to keep her ready for chartering. Chartering would not begin to defray her expenses and besides, not many people could afford to charter her for, at a minimum, $75,000 a week. By deciding to sell her, Bill Levitt reduced his cost of living by one million dollars a year, even if *La Belle* just sits in Majorca. How's that for an economy drive?

No matter what the economics involved, saying goodbye is not easy when you have loved a yacht as much as the Levitts loved *La Belle*. When they went to collect their clothes and favorite possessions and to bid adieu to their crew, Simone's eyes were not the only ones filled with tears. "If we just could have had one more summer— one more problemless summer," she said.

Captain Gotsch departed for Germany to enroll in nautical school where he could brush up on new yachting techniques and learn how to handle a "small" yacht of only 150 feet. When that smaller, swifter craft is launched, you can bet that somewhere in one of the old familiar places, Bill Levitt will find himself side by side with *La Belle Simone*. You can also bet that he will be the victim of mixed emotions when he sees her. It's not easy to be a prince when you have been a king. But knowing Bill, there will be that small but triumphant look in his eye. It's better to be a happy prince than a miserable king.

§

Another American tycoon, also considered adorable by some, is Kirk Kerkorian, the most unexpectedly soft-voiced, foot-dusting, aw-shucks tycoon in American captivity. Starting out as a scrap dealer in Fresno, California, his home town, Kirk went from enterprise to enterprise, each one more profitable than the preceding one. Kirk is now the money and the brains behind MGM. He was the creator and builder of the MGM Grand Hotel, which has the largest casino in Las Vegas, a city of large casinos, affording it a facility on a par with having one's own mint. Kirk has long been a friend of the beautiful people. He carts them around on his private 707, he doesn't drink or show his muscle, and whether he likes it or not, ladies find him devastating. Most of them take a flying run at him, but they rarely ruffle the surface of marital calm that reigns in the life of Jean Kerkorian, Kirk's wife, nor in the life of his two grown daughters. Kirk's idea of sport is tennis.

When Kerkorian decided to sell his 145-foot, 366-ton *Tracinda Jean* in Monte Carlo during the summer of 1972, he had better luck than Bill Levitt. He sold her all right, and quickly, in an even more dramatic fashion than he had bought her three years before. He sold her at auction on the high seas, and nobody had ever done that before. True, he had bought her at auction on dry land, but this second transaction was done in true Kerkorian style.

Tracinda Jean was well-known in Monte Carlo. She started life as John Bloom's *Ariane*, moved on to become Charles Revson's *Ultima I*, and then became *Kara Kara* under Ralph Stolkin's ownership. *Kara Kara* means "happy place" in South African, which she might have been for Stolkin, but only for two years. The U.S. Government took her over and put her on the auction block to gather some back tax money from Ralph Stolkin. Enter Kirk Kerkorian. He makes a grand entrance the same way Howard Hughes did—which is to say, he doesn't. That's left to the minions. The auction was held in Chicago, where a Kerkorian representative bid $900,000 for her and got her. Kirk promptly changed her name to *Tracinda Jean*, which combines the names of the three ladies he loves—his two daughters, Linda and Tracy, and his wife Jean. Original, no; sentimental, yes.

Actually, Kirk Kerkorian had no intention of buying a yacht. He wanted to charter, as he had before, but every single yacht he wanted to charter was taken that summer, so what the hell. What else was there to do but buy one? Jean Kerkorian had no wild desire to own a yacht either, but now that she had one, she wanted a marble bathroom to go with it. No one ever seems to buy a yacht and leave it alone. Expensive decorators appear the minute a yacht changes hands. Everything not latched down is moved, and everything latched down is redecorated. Presto! In no time flat, there was more beige Carrara marble aboard *Tracinda Jean* than you could shake a stick at. When the bathroom was ready, right down to the inevitable gold dolphin taps, everyone was ecstatic about it. Except the captain. The bathroom was so heavy that it tipped the yacht. Obviously, there was only one thing to do and it was done immediately. *Tracinda Jean* became the only yacht with matching beige marble bathrooms. The bathroom in the guest cabin on the port side of the yacht was just as impressive as the one in the master cabin on the starboard side. See what you can do if you put your mind to it? Even the captain was satisfied. No tilt.

Kirk Kerkorian kept *Tracinda Jean* for three years and enjoyed every moment that he spent aboard. He sent her to Cannes at Film Festival time. If some of his swinging young friends wanted to go to St. Tropez, he was happy to accommodate them, but he berthed her most often in Monte Carlo, his favorite tennis spot. Obviously, he likes tennis better than yachting. In three years he was aboard *Tracinda Jean* exactly eighteen times. When some of his highly paid accountants discovered that it cost him $80,000 for each twenty-four hours that he had spent on board, he decided to sell her. You can buy a lot of tennis balls for eighty grand.

Just as quickly as he had bought her, he put her up for auction, baffling the stuffy and nosy Monte Carloans. No one had ever done that before. Tongues began to wag, and when it became known that Peter Wilson was going to be her auctioneer, curiosity reigned supreme. Peter Wilson is probably the finest auctioneer in the world. He had banged down the gavel on some of the greatest goodies known to man for Sotheby's, the famous London-New York auction house, and he had seldom been caught with his bids down. "I've auctioned almost everything known to man," he said, "but this is the first time that I will ever have auctioned a yacht. On the high seas. I think it should be quite exciting."

It should have been, too. Invitations were hurriedly sent out to prospective buyers, and some forty accepted. They were still trying to figure out why Kirk Kerkorian wanted to get rid of his yacht so quickly. Same old questions. Was he broke? Was his marriage going sour? Was there something wrong with the yacht? To the nosy yacht-watchers, apparently no one has ever just plain wanted to sell a yacht for any other reason than a private personal disaster.

Most of the forty prospective buyers who came aboard *Tracinda Jean* were looking for a bargain. They were also looking for Kerkorian. He passed. The auction was set for four o'clock in the afternoon. That was Kirk's favorite time to play tennis, so he kept his tennis date.

Tracinda Jean came to a slow and stately stop five miles out to sea for the offshore auction, as determined by French law. Those aboard had guzzled some Dom Perignon and couldn't wait to see what was going to happen. It didn't take long. Peter Wilson had a table set up on deck, with a list of the potential buyers. He cleared his throat and said, "I have been commissioned to auction this yacht on behalf of Mr. Kirk Kerkorian." He then explained all of the yacht's vital statistics. When he finished, he said, "I have been advised to tell you that we will accept bids commencing with four hundred thousand dollars." Full stop.

And dead silence. Four hundred thousand dollars? That was no bargain, in the eyes of those aboard. They all knew that Kerkorian had paid $900,000 for her and put almost half of that again into her, but they had all read him wrong. He wasn't about to let *Tracinda Jean* be thrown to the bargain-hungry wolves, so he had instructed Peter Wilson to put what he considered a fair reserve price on her.

Everyone looked uncomfortably at everyone else. Peter Wilson repeated his short spiel. When there was still no bid, he said, "Since there are no bids, this auction is formally closed." No more than ten minutes had passed.

Tracinda Jean's engines started again. She made a slow, sweeping turn and headed back into port. The group aboard chatted in embarrassed tones, dying to get to shore and tell why they hadn't bid on *Tracinda Jean*. None would admit that they had expected to get a steal. Surprise, surprise. The word flew all over Monte Carlo. It even got to Kirk.

That evening, Kirk dined at Bec Rouge, one of Monte Carlo's best and most popular restaurants, with the friends who were his guests on *Tracinda Jean*. Everyone in town was there. Several people stopped at the table and said, "Too bad, Kirk," or "Sorry about that, Kirk." The enigmatic Mr. Kerkorian acknowledged the remarks, but said nothing. He excused himself before coffee and disappeared, alone, promising to rejoin his friends later.

Wherever he went that night, he moved in the right direction. When he rejoined his group, he said, "I've sold the yacht."

And he had. For $650,000. The buyer was Adnan Khashoggi, a long-time friend of Kirk's, who had chartered *Tracinda Jean* several times. Kerkorian and Khashoggi had made a deal before the auction at sea. Both men were sure that the yacht would go for more than $650,000. Khashoggi couldn't be bothered with going to the auction and that was the top price he wanted to pay. And a deal is a deal. When the yacht was not bid on, the deal between the two men still stood.

Khashoggi had no objections. He's bought several Kerkorian possessions, including a DC-9. And he is not a poor man. If you fiddle with his name, which is Saudi Arabian, it comes out Cash Today. (The cash part is easy, and "oggi" means "today" in Italian.) Besides a yacht and an airplane, his latest caprice is to build a fourth pyramid in Egypt as a monument to himself. The only difference between the Khashoggi pyramid and the old ones is that he plans to build his out of solid gold. What else?

Kirk Kerkorian's friends sipped a little more of the old bubbly and returned with him to the yacht. Adnan Khashoggi doesn't waste any more time than Kerkorian does. In the wee hours of the morning, Kerkorian woke a sleeping lawyer-friend of his who was occupying the cabin next to his own — the one with the matching marble bathroom. "Move," he said, grinning. "Khashoggi just came aboard and he's taken my cabin. He owns the yacht now." The lawyer moved to a lady friend's stateroom. But he didn't say, "Move." He said, "Move over." She grinned and moved over about four inches, wrapping her arms around the lawyer.

And so the tale of the sale had a happy ending. All four had made a move for the better.

15
Just
Leave It to
Charles

Ultima II, Charles Revson's 257-foot bow to status and success, was one of the great yachts in the Med from the time he bought her in the late Sixties until his death in 1975. *Ultima II*, originally *Danginn*, was built in Japan in 1960 by D.K. Ludwig, a far shyer multimillionaire than Revson, and one who really knew his yachts. He should, since he built some of the largest tankers in the world, as well as yachts. Everything that Ludwig had meticulously put together, including a crew of thirty-one Hong Kong Chinese, Okinawans, and a Portuguese captain, Charles Revson took over. For several million dollars.

Charles had cut his teeth on *Ariane*, a nice normal yacht that he bought from John Bloom and christened *Ultima I*. Charles Revson's taste rarely came under attack, but it did when he named his yacht *Ultima*. That was a little too commercial for the yachting world. "Why doesn't he just call it 'The Product'?" the snipers protested, but

154

nothing they said ruffled Revlon's founder for a second. Although he had no intention of repeating the expensive lessons he'd learned during the year he owned *Ultima I*, he did intend to use the name again.

Charles Revson started pouring nail polish out of buckets and into bottles in 1938, and from then on money poured back into the beauty empire he had built. Charles was a perfectionist, and life was not complete for him without the best yacht he could buy. He had decided to make business a pleasure and pleasure a business on his yacht, sometimes driving guests and employees alike right up the wall. But such is the way with perfectionists. Some men have yachts because they have nothing else to do. Charles had *Ultima II* because he had too much to do, and he wanted to do it all *his* way. On *Ultima II*.

Ultima II was his second choice for his second yacht. The one that really whet his whistle was Onassis' *Christina*. When Charles heard that *Christina* might be for sale, he had already put in a bid for *Danginn*, but he immediately set out to see if Onassis really wanted to sell. He did. Charles then spent $18,000 for a survey, sending a naval architect over every inch of *Christina*. When you start serious yacht-shopping, you can spend more on a survey than you would on a Rolls-Royce. When the survey proved satisfactory, Onassis made the next move. He invited Charles to join him on *Christina* in Bermuda for a few days of cruising. Charles had to decline for business reasons, so the two men met in the Onassis apartment in the Pierre Hotel instead.

"I couldn't tell, even then, if he was playing games with me just to see what I'd offer him for her," Charles said. "I knew what he had paid for the ship, and I knew that he'd spent close to a million and a half dollars converting her, but I had no idea what his price would be. It didn't take long. I offered him two and a half million, which he turned down flat. He wanted five million. I got the hell out of there, and when I got back to my office, my bid on *Danginn* had been accepted."

§

Mr. Revson, perfectionist at large, worked his new *Ultima II* over as if that already superior lily needed gilding. He replaced all her teak, provided her with new generators, and commissioned Ellen McClusky to completely refurnish her interiors. Ellen, who has decorated the inside of everything but a mummy case, and done it all superbly, lavished silks and satins and linens and tweeds on *Ultima II*, while Charles practically perched on her shoulder like a parrot, telling her what he wanted where. When she was done, *Ultima II* was a symphony of low-keyed luxury, cooly perfect.

Although there is no swimming pool and no auxiliary aircraft and no wood-burning fireplaces and no collection of old masters or impressionists, *Ultima II* does have every quality that a great yacht should, and she seems refreshingly like a yacht, rather than a floating hotel like a lot of others.

Charles wanted clear, clean colors on *Ultima II*, so Ellen McClusky obliged. Everything in the main salon, from couches to chairs to floors, was covered in sandstone beige and ivory. A few peacock-blue pillows were scattered about on the low couches and chairs. Glass and brass tables held beautiful objects. The lamps were blue and white porcelain, and the lighting was subtle and flattering. Charles wasn't in the beauty business for nothing.

The whole atmosphere screamed money—quietly. The dining room was a knockout. The walls were polished mahogany with deep, rich, red silk curtains at the windows and a flame-colored carpet. The chairs were Chinese lacquer. Masses of Charles's favorite red roses or carnations were piled into a Georgian silver centerpiece that cost more than an eighteen-foot Chris Craft. Charles's private quarters continued in the sandstone and beige color scheme. His sitting room was done in a tiny ivory and white stripe. Only the Telex machine chattering away in the corner brought you back to the realities of everyday business.

The guest cabins were more colorful. Ellen let herself go with color. She did up one of the eight double cabins in a blue fern pattern, another in tiny turquoise stripes, and a third one in a gorgeous coral toile de jouy. The yacht was full of built-in wood cabinets, to which Ellen added a French touch by adding molding to the existing woodwork and then painting the molding the predominant color of the cabin. The four single cabins were somewhat more masculine. The most dramatic of them had bright yellow walls, with curtains, bedspreads, and rug in a wild black and white plaid. Too noisy for Charles, but just right for a young bachelor. All in all, *Ultima II* made you feel as if you were spending a week or ten days at Claridge's, but the room service was much better.

§

Charles Revson and *Ultima II* spent seven years together. The summer of '71 ended on a high note with Earl Blackwell's beautiful Red and White Ball, which was given at the Hotel du Cap at Eden Roc, one of the world's most gorgeous watering places. Charles gave a seated dinner on *Ultima II* before the ball, and invited everyone who was anyone. It was one of those parties where things seemed to happen. Simone Levitt made her mark by showing up in Givenchy's white lace and sporting a matching eye patch that had a gardenia pinned to it to camouflage an eye injury. Liza Minnelli flew in from Spain, where she was making a film, to continue making eyes at Baron Alexis de Rede, her beau at the time. Rosemarie Kanzler met Jean Pierre Marci-Rivière, who turned out to be not only a handsome banker but also her future husband. The Paris group was there to a body—including the Edmond Borys and the Duchesse d'Uzes—all hating to say goodbye to the summer whirl. The Begum Aga Khan and Mary Lasker kept a snobbish and wary eye on everyone.

Every gentleman who didn't know what he was doing asked Lyn Revson to dance, not knowing that Lyn danced only to her husband's tune. Charles Revson would not allow his wife to dance with anyone. To compensate for this small idiosyncrasy, Charles bought the Norell enterprise, which included perfume, clothes, and everything else the great designer did. Lyn was allowed to deck herself out in Norman Norell masterpieces — slithery sequined garments that made it impossible for her to shake a leg anyway. Owning Norell took care of evening wear. The daytime atmosphere on *Ultima II* was strictly informal, with Charles and Lyn in perfectly tailored, identical shirts, which were ordered by the gross from Charles's shirtmaker in London.

In those early years, guests were taken everywhere and, by God, Charles saw to it that they saw what they were supposed to see. A lot of yacht guests have a valid complaint when the owner won't even let them go ashore long enough to run through the Doge's Palace in Venice, but not with Charles. He force-fed culture and history to his guests whether they liked it or not, and he did it magnificently. Jerome Zipkin, a sharp-witted perfectionist himself, spent several summers on *Ultima II*. "Newcomers aboard would ask me where we were going and when, and I'd say, 'Don't ask . . . just leave it to Charles.' While he would be in meetings with the executives he had flown in to wherever the yacht was, we would be meeting someone like Golda Meir, or flying over to Suez to be shown where the Six Day War had been fought. Charles arranged every detail perfectly; the chauffeurs and the charter planes and the very best guides and luncheons everywhere, all for our interest and comfort. I think the reason he stopped doing it was because so few friends really appreciated all the effort he made."

Even the crew knocked themselves out for you. Working for a perfectionist like Revson meant acquiring certain habits, and the members of the crew were nothing if not creatures of habit. If you ordered fresh grapefruit juice at ten-thirty in the morning, you got fresh grapefruit juice at ten-thirty *every* morning unless you called a halt. Some champagne at midnight? The next midnight on the dot, one of those sweet Chinese boys would find you and remind you that your champagne was chilled. It was almost automatic to gain ten pounds on any trip, since Charles unquestionably set the finest table that any yacht has even known. The Chinese food was superb. The French food was superb. The American food, including beef and chicken brought from Omaha and Long Island, was superb. All the food, and the wine as well, was superb. The only flaw was that Charles insisted on your enjoying every bite and every sip, or else.

When *Ultima II* was cruising, films were shown nightly, immediately after dinner. In the main salon the screen would drop down — but not as fast as the temperature of the room. Some like it cold, Charles said, but the simple fact was that *he* liked it cold. All you needed to get through the film was some Eskimo blood and four of the thick white Asprey blankets that were kept nearby. You'd be sunk down in a comfortable chair with your own personal Hong Kong boy behind your chair. He'd start you off with one blanket and then stand ready to bring others, or to rush you a brandy if your teeth chattered too loudly.

§

It was almost inevitable that Charles Revson and William J. Levitt would wind up in a feud. Charles had had the run of the Med for four years when Bill Levitt brought his new super yacht, *La Belle Simone*, into the competitive world of expensive yachting. The tongues wagged right away. Nothing is more fun than helping a feud along, and everyone held their breath, waiting to see how Charles Revson was going to handle the fantastic new competition, in the form of *La Belle Simone*, that now lay across the harbor from him. Charles ignored the new yacht. No one else did and they all chattered away about how big the two yachts were. *La Belle Simone* was wider than *Ultima II* but she was not as long. Bill Levitt mentioned quietly that if he had set out to build a bigger yacht than Charles Revson's, he obviously could have done so. The two self-made American tycoons were bound to tangle, although the only physical manifestation of it occurred one summer when they were berthed side by side and their anchors fouled, sealing the two yachts together for some uncomfortable hours.

Lyn Revson and Simone Levitt were casual friends and Bill Levitt is a friendly man, but Charles Revson just could not keep his perfectionist mouth shut. According to Charles, *La Belle Simone* was this, but not that; Simone Levitt knew nothing about food, the design of the yacht was imperfect, and so on. Pretty soon everyone was up tight. The Levitts and Revsons stopped inviting each other to their parties, and they stayed shooting-distance away from each other at other parties. All of this was much to the distress of three of the four of them. Then Bill Levitt unwittingly widened the rift. He added eighteen feet to the afterdeck of *La Belle Simone*. There had been rumors that he planned to crack the yacht in two and add four guest suites for kings and presidents, but these were unfounded. Bill Levitt had learned by then that he wanted no more than the eight guests he could already accommodate, and to hell with presidents and kings. Let them fend for themselves. However, there was a basic improvement to be made in the design of *La Belle Simone*. With eighteen feet added to the stern, the yacht would be stabilized and a much-needed arrival deck could be added. It was so done. *La Belle* and *Ultima II* were now the same length but Levitt's lady was wider. Oh, dear heaven, the to-do it all caused. Certainly, if Charles Revson had been gracious and not so sharply critical from the beginning, all would have been sweetness and light. But Charles was riding high, wide, handsome and difficult.

Earl Blackwell, who cruised on *Ultima II* for all seven of her summers, understood Charles Revson better than did a great many of his employees. In Marbella when Earl was going ashore, he asked Charles if he wanted him to invite some friends for cocktails the next evening. "Yes," said Charles. "Invite whomever you like and tell them to come at six." When Earl returned, Charles asked who would be coming on board and Earl said, "No one." "Why not?" asked Charles. "Because I didn't invite anyone. This is Spain," Earl said, "and no one would think of coming to cocktails before nine o'clock." He knew that if he had corrected Charles about time earlier, there would have been an eruption. The perfectionist was not to be challenged. "Well, if you had just said so," said Charles impatiently. "Ask whomever you like to come tomorrow night and tell them to be here at nine."

The guest list in the early years was fifty percent Social Register and fifty percent *Hollywood Reporter*, with massive numbers of Revlon executives thrown in. More and more, the latter appeared as the years went by. Merle Oberon and her industrialist husband, Bruno Pagliai, were frequent guests, as were the Marquesa Carroll de Portago, the Denniston Slaters, and Jane Pickens Langley. It was all very exciting then, but gradually Charles began to demand too much of his guests. His whim was law. Eight friends would arrive in Monte Carlo, bright-eyed, bushy-tailed, and ready to go. Charles wouldn't tell them where they were going or if, in fact, they *were* going anywhere. The port of Monte Carlo is for yachts but it is not for yachting. Gradually, fewer and fewer of the eight double and four single cabins were filled. Gradually, almost every guest was a Revlon employee. *They* never seemed to turn down his invitations.

Although Charles Revson loved *Ultima II* and he ran it magnificently, he might have been a happier and less lonely man if he had been a guest instead of a host. He knew how to behave only one way. His way. He understood and achieved a power known to few men. On *Ultima II* he was all-powerful. And, during the last summer, all alone.

16
The
New
Yachting

Joe E. Lewis said it all in that one line: "You only live once, but if you work it right, once is enough." Working it right in yachting in these fast-moving last decades of the twentieth century involves entirely different ground rules than ever before.

In the old days you had to be rich and old in order to "work it right." Now you still have to be rich, but you'd better be young. Under fifty. Under forty. With any luck, you haven't even hit thirty-five. In other words, your vital statistics should be like those of the new yachts themselves; the numbers are getting shorter, not longer. The magic number for a yacht's footage is one hundred or less, and you cut that number in half—or even in thirds—to figure the age of the yacht's owner. The real players these days are a young bunch. Onassis is gone, Niarchos is an old man, and even the Aga Khan is a bit over the hill.

Naturally, you have made your own fortune, and it's a large one. It is much better to have a rags-to-riches background in this phase of our civilization. Today, names like Morgan and Astor and Vanderbilt conjure up some old-fashioned magic of time past, but nothing more. In those days, in order to even consider having a yacht, a man had to have "background." Background consisted of a super-snobbish name, tons of dough, and a lifetime subscription to the New York Social Register, which you never got thrown out of. The yachting gentleman had social and financial power — and, baby, more often than not he had inherited both. It would have been downright socially unacceptable for the man you bought your motor cars from to have a yacht, be it motor or sail. You could row, row, row your boat if you were the common man, but not within spitting distance of the New York Yacht Club you couldn't. My, how times have changed. Now there are a whole passel of young, self-made yachters all over the best watering places, having a wonderful time and not wishing for a moment that you, Sir, were here.

If you have made your own fortune, speak three languages, are Austrian with an American passport, have a beautiful young wife, a collection of some eighteen to twenty vintage cars (not counting the cream Bentley and the white Rolls-Royce in your Palm Springs garage), two houses, two apartments, two dogs, three cats, five servants, your second helicopter (plus license to fly it), your fifth Lear jet (painted bright red, and naturally you fly it, too) and, on top of it all, your fifth yacht — one that goes like a bat out of hell — your name might well be John von Neumann. It would have to be. There's only one man who fits that description, and only one John von Neumann.

He's working it right. Although John von Neumann was born in Vienna as the son of Baron Heinrich von Neumann, his fortune was made in America. That's not to say that the titled Daddy von Neumann didn't have money, but he didn't have a lot of it. The chief riches he passed on to his son was the knowledge that money was important. John von Neumann, by some superior mathematics, worked his way up and out of a garage in Hollywood to become the Volkswagen-Porsche dealer for the entire Southwestern part of America. He worked like a dog from 1953 until 1973. Then he decided to work it right — and he retired. That's one of the ground rules of the new image, too: Retire before the silver hits the hairline. He has a perfect desire never to work at anything else again, except his hobbies. He intends to enjoy life as long as it and he are around, and it's more than a fair bet that the century will run out sooner than he will.

§

Consider this lifestyle for a moment — and remember that a yacht, yachts, and yachting are a paramount part of it.

Start with *Cochise*, John's present — and fifth — yacht. *Cochise* is not only under one hundred feet long, it's *way* under one hundred feet. *Cochise* is sixty-eight feet of gray glory, modeled on an Italian torpedo boat, and so avant garde that you have to see it to believe it. Even that is easier said than done, since *Cochise* is painted peacetime Mediterranean gray, and half the time you can't see her even when she's right there in front of you. She has a fadeaway, slightly sinister look about her, even in the daytime, and her gray coat gives her that eerie capacity to camouflage herself. Also, she is one yacht that should never be called she. Even Ms. would be risky with *Cochise*. She looks like an aggressive, fast-moving man. She looks a little bit like John von Neumann. So much for *Cochise*, for the moment.

Cleo and John von Neumann spend their winters in Mexico and in their comfortable house in Palm Springs, California. The rest of the time they are in Europe, where they have an apartment in Geneva and another in St. Tropez. They also have a house in Beverly Hills, but they are both crazy about the house in Palm Springs. It's an unshowy house, for all their material possessions, and they are actually unshowy people. Dutch-born, Indonesian-raised Cleo is spectacularly beautiful and John is spectacularly successful, but regardless of all the trappings, they have an aura of the-folks-next-door about them. Next door

164

could be the Getty Museum, but the Von Neumanns have their camouflage, just the way *Cochise* has.

It takes John less than a split second to get to the business at hand, and when he does, Cleo jumps right in, too. In the double conversation they never bicker or contradict each other, and although it is easy to hear what both of them are saying at the same time, it's hard to absorb all of what they say. Their world is so strewn with speed and life and yachts and planes and cats and dogs and travel, and the style is so natural to them, that you get this sort of "doesn't everybody live this way?" feeling from them. Everybody doesn't. Hardly anyone does.

"In the summer of '62 I chartered a perfectly conventional English yacht and we made the regular twenty-five cent tour of the Mediterranean for a very big price," John says, pawing through some drawings of yachts on the table in front of him. Cleo, meanwhile, wearing an orange bikini, has curled up with one of the cats in a large wing chair while John continues. "The whole thing was an old-fashioned pain in the neck. The yacht was too big and too slow. We had nothing but crew problems, as there were too many of them and they had nothing to do. The captain was either drunk or about to get drunk. Or he was having a nervous breakdown. He didn't have the charts to go where I wanted to go or else he was afraid to go where I wanted to go. It was a disaster, that trip. But one day in a port somewhere, my eye caught a glimpse of a beautiful boat. I began to think about it later, but the next day it was gone. In another port, I thought I saw it again. As the weeks went by, I kept catching a glimpse of it, and then I realized that it was not one boat but that there were many of them. They were Bagliettos, made in Italy, and there were lots of them around.

"One day I found one lying alongside us and I asked the captain if I could have a look. I liked everything I saw, so in September I went to the Baglietto place near Genoa and I ordered a standard 55-foot Ischia, which became the *JvNI*. (John von Neumann I). All my boats are *JvN*'s, and have their own names as well. Anyhow, since I like to fiddle with mechanical things, I started making changes right away. *Cochise* is the fifth Baglietto I've owned, but I've made her very different from that first one. *Cochise* looks like a warship, and she should, being a private variation of a torpedo boat and named after a renegade. Before her, I had *Geronimo*, named after the Apache chief, and the new boat next year will be named *Tazah* after the brother of Cochise."

He came to a pause, but not for long.

"To me, a boat is not a house. It's a vehicle. A vehicle of speed. I want to have lunch in Italy and dinner in France. *Cochise* does a maximum of 41.7 knots and she cruises point to point at 37 knots. It takes me five hours and twenty minutes to go from St. Tropez to Porto Rotondo. I have a captain and a sailor. The captain cooks."

Cleo chimes in. "We have room on board for three in crew but it never works. Everyone hates the third, so it's usually two and that's plenty."

John goes on. "I think the hull is the most beautiful part of a boat, and everything that can be, should be in the hull. What superstructure you have is therefore light, and that's where your speed comes from. When *Tazah* is built, she'll have an aluminum hull rather than a wooden one like *Cochise*, making her lighter and even faster. She'll probably be turbine-powered.

"Her living quarters won't be any different. What we have now is perfect for us. We only sleep four, in two double cabins (including Cleo's and mine), and we have queen size beds, since no one is really comfortable in bunks. And another thing. We don't have one of those gladiola back deck arrangements, if you know what I mean. Our living quarters are amidships. The crew sleeps forward and the galley and engines are aft. How many times have you sat on the aft deck of a yacht in port and had the delicious smell of the crew's garlic soup wafting under your nose, and the fumes of the engine adding to the stench?

"We have a bar in the big salon, and the guest quarters are the equivalent of a studio apartment, just off the main salon. There's no door between, just a sliding leather partition for privacy when someone is staying aboard. Otherwise it opens up as part of the salon, with a Gucci fur throw on the bed. There are two full-size bathrooms and plenty of dressing room space and a sauna."

Cleo stands up and stretches her lissome body. "We don't often have people stay with us on the boat. We cruise alone with the dogs. We have a lot of friends, but not that many close friends. People join us for two or three days at most wherever we are. What's fun is to rendezvous with other yachts and go off on trips together."

§

A recent rendezvous caused a memorable fracas. It seems that *Cochise* carries two cannons and some smoke-screen laying equipment. The cannons are the type used on many yachts, small noisemakers used to celebrate anniversaries or birthdays or to greet royalty with the good old 21-gun salute. It's not the kind of artillery to provoke a battle — unless you use it as John and Cleo did.

Cochise crossed paths with Gunther Sachs, who is a full-time international playboy and part-time yacht charterer. Gunther loves being the biggest shot of all wherever he goes, and he had chartered *Amazone,* one of the better yachts available, to establish his status on this cruise. John and Cleo decided to tease him by throwing out a smoke screen to hide his fat-cat yacht, and at the same time firing the "cans," as they call them, in the air. Sachs can dish it out, but he surely didn't take it; his age and nature are a combustible combination. Sachs chased the Von Neumanns in a pair of fast Rivas, shooting live flares at them. Oh, what games these hot-blooded bucks do play. Live flares are dangerous, and although *Cochise* escaped unharmed, the nearby island of Porquerolles did not. Then the Coast Guard got into the act and made Sachs and his crew put out the forest fire they had started in the pine trees. Relations between the Sachs and Von Neumann camps have been strained since then, to say the least.

"Not everyone likes us," says Cleo, with becoming candor. "Sam Spiegel can live without us. We were testing the 'cans' one day and fired one when we passed Sam cruising with some of his old friends. They all fell off the lunch table."

The Von Neumann apartment in St. Tropez is just above L'Escale, a restaurant at the end of the port. The Von Neumanns leave seasonal clothes there, and keep their guests there. "All I have to do is yell out the window for my captain," John says. "We take the boat and go. Last summer we rendezvoused with Michael Pearson on *Hedonist* in Trieste, and we came all the way down the coast of Yugoslavia together. Every day, we would take off and wait for Michael to catch up. It makes him mad that we're so much faster. We hardly ever go at night. One summer we spend our time in the eastern part of the Med and the next we will go all over the western part. *Cochise* has a range of 500 nautical miles and the Med is about 1,500 miles long. It's easy for me to run nonstop from Genoa, which is the most important big port in the Med, to Marbella on Spain's Costa del Sol."

For all their love of speed and the very latest things, it seems incongruous that both Cleo and John go into raptures about a not-so-modern Egyptian friend of theirs, Michael Fayed, who lives in London. He owns the *Dodi*, an enormous sailing yacht that was built in Seattle around 1900. But it's not the yacht that appeals to the Von Neumanns, it's the style of life. "He lives in complete Middle Eastern splendor," they say, both talking at the same time again. "There are exotic embroidered cushions and tentlike hangings all over the place, and walls of patent leather. The crew of *Dodi* is Italian, except for Michael's personal valet and he is Egyptian, as black as night, and has those frightening scars carved on his cheeks."

The *Dodi* is a two-masted schooner, and apparently Michael Fayed keeps it splendidly. When he bought her, he spent more than half a million dollars decorating and air conditioning her. Cleo is talking now. "He has the best food on any yacht anywhere. I suppose it's Sudanese, but whatever it is, there's no yacht anywhere that I would rather be invited to dine on."

"The exotic background is attractive, but I don't

want her," John remarks. "It takes her four hours to go where we go in fifteen minutes, but then, I like speed, and Michael cares nothing about it."

§

Them what has gets things done. Cleo and John start their annual peregrination to Europe in early June. The two dogs sit waiting patiently for the suitcases to be closed. They know they are part of the package, and they can't wait to get going. You might know that the Von Neumanns wouldn't have your run-of-the-mill mutt, and they don't. The two dogs are Xoloitzcuintlis. In case you care to try to pronounce that, try "show-low-eats-queen-tlees." Just try it. Otherwise, call them Xolos. Cleo is trying to save the near-extinct breed. These dogs have been around since 1500 B.C., and they look it. They are standard Mexican hairless, no relation at all to Chihuahuas except in being hairless, and they are black and evilly aristocratic-looking beasts. Naturally, they swim well and are great yachters.

The warmed-up red Lear jet is waiting with the co-pilot for instant takeoff from Palm Springs. One more stop, and then they touch down in Geneva. They stay there for a week or so, and then it's off to St. Tropez and *Cochise*. John flies into the airport, La Mole. "It's only twenty minutes from the port at St. Tropez. Before, there was only a grass runway which was too short for the Lear, so I had them lengthen and pave it for me, and build a hangar for the plane." Of course he did.

The Yugoslav captain and the Spanish sailor greet them, and everyone but the dogs prattles happily on in French, which is the only language they share. The refugee captain escaped from his homeland by rowing across the Adriatic to Italy, and finally got French citizenship. The sailor's history is undramatic. John picked him up in Majorca one day three years before and he's been with them ever since.

"I don't belong to any yacht club," John remarks. "When I first bought the boat, I thought of course one must belong to a yacht club somewhere, so I decided to join the Yacht Club Italiano, since I was buying and building and spending a lot of money on boats in Italy. But I had to go to Rome to apply, and I had to meet and be approved by Count So-and-So and Prince Whatzisname. I'm not saying that they looked down their noses at me, but I am saying that I could be dead and long gone before they would decide to take me in as a member. I haven't got time for that sort of thing in any part of my life, and belonging to a yacht club means nothing to me."

By the time one yacht is well broken in, John has another on the drawing board. "I normally have a new yacht every two years. It takes a year to plan one and a year to build one. There are such rapid advances in yacht design that it doesn't pay to try to keep up with them by revamping your old yacht. It only makes sense to build a new one."

§

The apartment in St. Tropez has been opened up and is waiting for the Von Neumanns to unpack their bags, arrange for their guests, and take off. Three months of summer stretch ahead of them. A few days in St. Tropez, then to Monte Carlo for an eating binge. They go to Bec Rouge, the best restaurant in Monte Carlo, and they frequent the elegantly old-fashioned terrace of the Hôtel de Paris to have a marvelous dinner. "Everyone is seventy, at least," Cleo says. "But the scene is lovely and somehow just right for Monte Carlo with all the old ladies wearing their beautiful jewels." Still eating, they go up the Moyenne Corniche to the Chateau Madrid, or over to Voile d'Or in St. Jean-Cap Ferrat. At least once a summer they stop at Le Pirate, the wild restaurant on the sea near Menton. Here, everyone goes crazy and throws tables, chairs, and everything else not bolted down, into the fire. *Cochise* docks there shooting off her cannons, so it's six of one and half a dozen of the other as to who is the most obstreperous. The Pirate who owns the place charges as if the rustic wooden chairs and tables were Louis Seize, but it's a must at least once a summer.

Cleo and John are natural sophisticates. When most people wander off into the sunset, it is because they are old and bored with life. When the Von Neumanns head out into the sunset, *Cochise* seems to fairly jump out of the harbor. She is cracking along at 37 knots in no time at all. The captain and sailor are smiling. The dogs are rushing about wagging their tails. None of them looks back, not even to wave. They are too busy looking ahead.

17
Emily and the Swan

Once upon a time, there was a lady whose name was Emily Roebling. She was very rich and very pretty and her granddaddy built the Brooklyn Bridge, among other things. Emily grew up and got married, but she was never going to be your average housewife—not in any way. She married Richard Cadwallader, who was a Cadwallader of Philadelphia, and she loved yachts.

Emily was a romantic type and she had once read a Chinese fairy tale about a beautiful princess who loved a swan. The swans in that part of China were known as savarona birds, and Emily knew that if she ever did have a yacht she would name it *Savarona* after the exotic Chinese swan. She discussed the matter with her husband, having by this time decided that she was going to build a yacht. "Whatever you want, my dear," said Mr. Cadwallader. "It's your money."

So Emily built a beautiful 174-foot yacht and christened it *Savarona*. All of Emily's friends were thrilled, and Mr. Cadwallader was fond of the yacht, too. But Emily had gone even further—she had fallen head over heels in love with yachting, and soon the day came when she wanted a much bigger yacht. "By all means, darling," said Mr. Cadwallader. "It's your money."

Savarona II was a real dazzler. Emily was ecstatic and so were her friends and so was Mr. Cadwallader. The new *Savarona II* was 294 feet long and she was equipped with gyrostabilizers, which were fairly new on yachts at that time. Gyrostabilizers kept the ship from rocking too much when the weather was rough. *Savarona*'s handsome chief engineer told Emily that a funny thing about the stabilizers was that, although they kept things smooth in rough water, if they were turned on in smooth water they *made* the boat rock. "Really!" said Emily, clapping her hands. "What fun! Turn them on." So the handsome engineer turned on the stabilizers whenever Emily had guests on board for cocktails and everyone had a marvelous time on *Savarona II*, rocking happily away in the harbor.

By this time, Emily Cadwallader was even more in love with yachts and yachting. She was also extremely competitive and she had long ago become very used to having her own way. It made her miserable—in fact it destroyed a whole season for her—when she discovered that Julius Forstmann's *Orion* was 333 feet long and, worse yet, that J.P. Morgan's *Corsair* was 343 feet long. This would never do. It took all the fun out of having little old 294-foot *Savarona II* when all anybody ever talked about was *Orion* or *Corsair*.

Emily Cadwallader decided to build the biggest and best yacht in the whole world, bigger and better than anyone else ever had or ever would. She'd show them. "Of course, sweetheart," said Mr. Cadwallader. "It's your money." This time, Mr. Cadwallader really said a yachtful.

§

Savarona III was and is, to this day, the biggest and probably the most beautiful private yacht ever built. Stavros

Niarchos' *Atlantis* is only 380 feet long. Don't you love that "only"? The Queen of England's *Britannia* is 412 feet long, but was built as a hospital ship rather than a private yacht. Length is not everything, but the fact remains that Emily Cadwallader and Marjorie Post, two American women, still hold the track record for owning the two largest private yachts ever built. It says a little something for the ladies' spirits, as well as their incomes.

Statistics can quickly put us all to sleep unless they're making money for us, but *Savarona III*'s were superlative. She cost $4 million to build in 1931. When the Blohm & Voss shipyards in Hamburg sent *Savarona III* down the ways, she measured 408 feet in length and weighed 4,646 tons. Her cruising range was 6,000 miles and she clipped along at a speed of 18 knots. There were eighty-nine men in her crew, although she could accommodate one hundred. There were eight spare rooms for other people's maids and valets. About one-third of *Savarona III*'s crew were officers, and all of her officers were American. Including the handsome chief engineer.

Emily Cadwallader tried to keep her plans for the building of *Savarona III* quiet, but it was impossible. Headline stories appeared everywhere. "World's Largest Yacht Prepared for Launching," said one. "Five Million Dollar 'Yacht of Mystery' Built for U.S. Owner in Hamburg," said another. It wasn't long before Emily Cadwallader was tracked down as the lady who had commissioned the building of the largest yacht in the world. She was unavailable for comment. Her husband and William Francis Gibbs, the yacht's designer, were unavailable for comment, and Captain H.C. Fish, who had relinquished command of the *Republic*, the fourth largest vessel in the American Merchant Marine, in order to guide *Savarona III* along her merry way, refused to utter a word. Emily even stayed discreetly away when the yacht was launched — although she had driven a rivet into the hull when building started — and *Savarona III*'s hull received the crack of the champagne bottle at the hand of Mrs. Blohm, wife of the German shipyard owner.

Regardless of the why-the-hell-shouldn't-she-do-what-she-wants-with-her-money attitude of a few, public feeling about *Savarona III* and Emily Cadwallader ran high for a time. The year 1931 might have been a normal year for the lady with the big yacht, but the rest of the United States was experiencing a major depression. It was bad enough that Emily had deprived Americans of hundreds of jobs by building the leviathan of a yacht in Germany, but she added fuel to the fire when they sent a model of *Savarona III* on a tour of several European countries. An impoverished king saw it and wrote to Emily, offering to sell her a porcelain dinner service for one hundred if she would simply forward him a check for $25,000. He remarked that she was the only person he had heard of who could possibly afford it. She refused his kind offer but, for possibly the first time, her wealth was an embarrassment to her.

§

The Cadwalladers took *Savarona III* on a shakedown cruise to the Scandinavian countries. Although she could accommodate twenty-four guests, Emily never invited more than half that number to cruise with them. With that few guests, the eighty-nine in crew would have been falling all over themselves if they hadn't had carefully portioned-out duties. Somehow, the captain and the staff captain kept them all busy.

Emily Cadwallader had commissioned Morgan Cromwell Wells to make her super-swan's interiors as glorious as could be. Morgan Wells had decorated Emily's house, and there was no reason he couldn't handle her yacht too. As it turned out, he handled the yacht much the same way he might have handled her home, because both Mrs. Cadwallader and Morgan Wells preferred palatial to nautical trappings. They both leaned toward the Louis'— Fourteenth, Fifteenth, and Sixteenth. Why they couldn't settle for one Louis is uncertain unless Emily's more-is-better syndrome covers this, too. At any rate, Morgan Wells spent more than a year in Paris having *Savarona III*'s furnishings made. Reproductions were ordered, since no one in his right mind would expose true antiques to sea air.

Just to give you an idea of Emily's style, her bedroom and sitting room covered the width of the yacht, and she also had two bathrooms, a dressing room, a room for her personal maid, and her own private stairway to the deck above. Morgan Wells did one of her bathrooms in black marble, and the taps were, of course, golden swans. The chef made swans out of ice as table decorations for parties. A great silver swan, usually filled with roses and lilies, was the centerpiece on the dining room table. You were up to your ears in swans.

There was a grand staircase for grand entrances or exits, but regardless of the grandness of it all, Emily actually ran a fairly informal ship. No one dressed for dinner. Emily fancied rather tailored clothes and the gentlemen wore blazers but never black tie. Although the dining table seated twenty-four, a smaller table in a corner of the dining room was the one most frequently used. It was cozier that way. The little table seated only ten.

§

Savarona III, sadly, was not long for Emily Cadwallader's world. It was impossible to bring her to America, for her import taxes could not have been paid, even by an Emily Cadwallader. She never got closer than Bermuda, and Emily made only three trips on her. The first was her shakedown cruise to the Scandinavian countries. When that ended and the last guests departed, Emily and Richard, accompanied only by Morgan Cromwell Wells, crossed the Atlantic to Bermuda. "It was a quiet but lovely crossing," Morgan Wells remembers. "Richard and I would be up for breakfast. We would read the ship's newspaper that was printed for us daily, containing just the highlights of what had come over the radio from London or Paris or New York. Emily never appeared for breakfast. The three of us would meet for a cocktail before lunch, and after lunch we would all disappear to read or write. Then we'd meet for a drink before dinner."

Richard Cadwallader voiced only one opinion of *Savarona III*, and even that was stated indirectly. "It's your money, my love," he said. "But you know we had the best time of all on that first massive overblown houseboat of yours." He was referring to *Savarona I*, Emily's first crack at yachting, which has now become *Sequoia*, our very own presidential yacht. When the Cadwalladers arrived in Bermuda, a group of friends and curious yachtsmen who were dying to see *Savarona III* had arrived there just to see Emily's famous yacht. Shortly afterwards, the Cadwalladers went home to Philadelphia, and *Savarona III* went back to Hamburg for maintenance and repairs.

The following year the Cadwalladers took a long trip to the Caribbean and South America and, again, at the end of it, *Savarona III* returned to Hamburg.

She stayed there. Emily Cadwallader was ill and her super-swan was for sale. It wasn't long before the Hitler group came running. Just the thing for Adolf, who must have the best of everything. Emily Cadwallader was not too ill to give the Germans a snappy turndown. The next offer interested her. The Turkish government wanted *Savorona III* as a state yacht for Ataturk. Emily was sold on what Ataturk was achieving in his country, so she sold *Savarona III* to the Turkish government for a reputed one million dollars. She made two provisions. The yacht was never to go into trade, and her name was not to be changed. The Turks got their hands on her and changed her name to *Gunes Dil* faster than you could say "sea tongue," which is what the name meant. But the paint was hardly dry on her new name before Ataturk stepped in and said, "The name of this yacht is *Savarona*," and that was that. He did drop III, but that was because the swan was only *his* first.

The dictator spent even less time on board than Emily Cadwallader had, and for the same reason. Ataturk had been ill for some time but his health now failed rapidly, and after no more than fifty days on *Savarona*, he died. *Savarona* then became, and still is, a training ship for the Turkish navy and she has been kept in excellent condition. In the foyer there is a photograph of Mrs. Blohm, wife of the shipyard owner, and above it, set into a small niche, is the head of the bottle of champagne that Mrs. Blohm used to christen *Savarona III* in those dear, dead, luxurious days of the past. There are no mementos or photographs of Emily Cadwallader anywhere, although the Turkish officers think that Mrs. Blohm is "Miss Cadwallader," as they refer to her, and they squabble among themselves as to who gets to use "Miss Cadwallader's" black marble bathtub first.

The romantic Turks will try to tell you that Emily had a love affair with the handsome chief engineer and, to prove it, they show you the secret passage that leads from his quarters to hers. Emily's unromantic nephew, Gouverneur Cadwallader, Jr., will tell you that the tiny private room that the Turks point to was Emily's maid's room, but he says so with regret. "I wish I thought it was true," he says. "My aunt was gay and romantic and she was never angry with anyone, but even so, any liaison that she might have had with him would have been brief. After all, she had less than two years on *Savarona III*."

Would that she had had longer. If you look carefully at the plans of *Savarona III*, you will see that the private stairway that led from Emily's quarters to the deck above comes out in front of a door. The door leads, by design or chance, to the quarters that were assigned to the chief engineer. Perhaps Emily Cadwallader was living a fairy tale of her own.

18
A Dream,
a Queen and
a Floating
Palace

The only thing bluer than the Queen of England's blue, blue blood is the color of her magnificent yacht, *Britannia.* To say that either is truly royal blue would be inaccurate. The Queen is a remarkably red-blooded lady who works longer hours than any stevedore, and *Britannia* is navy blue, not royal.

The two of them spend a lot of time together to the mutual enjoyment of both, but it is a feeling not necessarily shared by some of the grumpy British taxpayers who foot the bill for the yacht's intensive travel schedule. Anyhow, they do foot it, and they cannot complain that *Britannia* is used for anything but the exhausting business of monarchy.

The Queen of England is crazy about her yacht. She does not own it—the Ministry of Defense does—but she might as well, as she spends more time aboard than most men spend in their offices. It would be awful, wouldn't it, to think how boring life would be for Her Majesty if she hated the sea, got seasick, or thought of her yacht as a great big bore? But Elizabeth II has none of those weaknesses. She has lived aboard *Britannia* for months at a time, and traveled for hundreds of thousands of miles in really regal splendor, going about her queenly business. When *Britannia* pulls into port anywhere in the world, the Royal Standard flying, to see her is to believe that the Queen and Britannia still rule the waves.

Neither of them waives the rules, however, not anywhere they happen to be. Protocol on the royal yacht is as splendid as it should be, and guests invited aboard are usually as excited as children. The yacht makes even more of an impression on them than Buckingham Palace does. They are in awe of *Britannia* and they know they are the cat's meow when they are presented to the Queen by her Equerry, and then passed swiftly down the long line of those who are there to take care of them.

The Royal Yacht has been criticized for the simple reason that it has cost the British taxpayer over $20 million to operate over the last twenty years. Certain taxpayers consider Buckingham Palace, the Royal Yacht, and the whole expense and largesse of monarchy both an anachronism and an unnecessary expense. Twenty million dollars does seem like a lot of money, but it has covered the cost of pay and allowances for her seemingly innumerable crewmen, her fuel, supplies, maintenance, and minor refits for twenty years now. I don't know what those taxpayers are yapping about, for these expenses break down to approximately one million dollars a year. It has cost a whole flock of other yachtsmen almost as much as that just to straggle through one long Mediterranean summer and one short Caribbean winter, with only half the pomp and none of the circumstance.

Besides, *Britannia* is a special case. First of all, she is too huge to really be thought of as a yacht. She is 412 feet long, she weighs 5,769 tons, and she looks longer and heavier than that. She moves along at 21 knots, which is a pretty fast clip for that large a lady. She was planned from the very beginning, in 1952, to play two distinct roles. In a peaceful world, she would be the Royal Yacht, but if war came again she could quickly be converted into a small hospital ship. Being basically a hospital ship, she was meant to be as stable as a carpenter's level; her air conditioning could freeze you solid on a summer day in Death Valley, and her laundry facilities would thrill a sea-going laundryman. The after end of the sun deck can be, and is, used for helicopter landings, and that works just as well for a queen as it does for an outpatient.

Britannia's private and the state apartments are decorated with some furniture taken from the *Victoria and Albert*, the gorgeous former royal yacht. The Queen launched *Britannia* in April of 1953. She took two years to build and cost £2,098,000, one of the only nondebatable figures available on the cost of any yacht, anywhere, anytime.

§

Life aboard *Britannia* is quite unlike life aboard any other yacht, royal or no. Naturally, it has its upstairs-downstairs quality. *Britannia's* captain is the only Admiral of the Fleet who is captain of a ship. She carries a complement of 21 officers and, catch this, 242 crew members. The crewmen's uniforms are dark blue or white jumpers, depending on the occasion, tucked into trousers that are finished off in the back with a black silk bow. *Britannia's* crew are chic as the devil, probably because of that immense laundry space. They were a swinging crew, too, until the yacht's major refit in 1972. Swinging in hammocks. *Britannia* was the last ship in the Royal Navy that slept a flock of her men in hammocks. The thought of the Queen of England tucked up in her big, pale blue silk double bed and snoozing away on one deck while her seamen swung in hammocks several decks below her is delicious. But, thank heaven the refit changed all that. The boys are resplendent in bunks now.

Britannia was busy in the late Sixties and the early Seventies or her major refit would have been carried out long before. She is an extremely active lady, always on the go, and not just with the Queen as her mistress. She is officially used by most working members of the Royal Family, and most members of the Royal Family work, believe it or not, at Royalty. Elizabeth, the Queen Mother, cruises the West Indies on royal business, and Princess Margaret spent her honeymoon aboard when she was plain Mrs. Anthony Armstrong-Jones and her husband had not yet become Lord Snowdon. The Princess Royal makes offical voyages, too, and in the good old summertime the Royal Family gathers together for a summer cruise up the West Coast of Scotland en route to Balmoral. During that time *Britannia* is a real family yacht, showing her most informal colors. Prince Edward and Prince Andrew invite some of their school friends, and Princess Anne and Prince Charles show up every year for "the family trip."

All yachts are thought of as "floating palaces," but *Britannia* is literally just that. Other mortals have to find fuel, and a yacht owner no longer just pulls into port and says, "Fill 'er up"; he goes where fuel is, when it is available. Not *Britannia*. Fuel comes to her wherever she is, provided politely by a ship of the Royal Navy. Massive trappings of royalty are aboard *Britannia*, some in the form of additional transport. There are boats on boats on boats aboard, and most of them are larger than your neighbor's biggest "yacht." There is a 41-foot royal barge, and even an inflatable raft that can carry a Land Rover ashore when necessary. The Queen uses the Land Rover more often than she uses the two Rolls-Royces that are stashed below, but the Rolls-Royces are there in case she travels to one of her poorer dominions where she might be forced into something unroyal.

The entourage traveling with the Queen on long Royal Tours is as impressive as can be. The Queen and Prince Philip are accompanied by various members of the Royal Household. Within the group there is the Private Secretary to the Queen, the Equerry to the Queen, and the Lady-in-Waiting to the Queen. On long trips there will be two Ladies-in-Waiting to the Queen. They wear out faster than she does. The Queen's personal maid and hairdresser are aboard and are available to the Lady- or Ladies-in-Waiting as well as to Her Majesty. Prince Philip brings his Private Secretary and his own Equerry—and his personal valet, so he doesn't have to leave his shoes outside the door of the Royal Bedroom. Then there is the Master of the Royal Household and the Press Secretary—and they have secretaries of their own.

§

Buckingham Palace goes right along with the Queen on the long tours. The footmen and pages are in their royal red livery, and the chief chef is in his galley planning the evening's meal. Her majesty's favorite Malvern water is cooling in the fridge, and her home-away-from-home is intact, even to the family doctor. The Royal corgis cannot go cruising, but they're the only members of the Royal household left behind. England has a six months quarantine law governing the entry of animals into the United Kingdom, and even the Queen must respect that law.

The anteroom, a sort of a pre-parlor where the Queen receives, and the drawing room beyond are both deceptively chintzy and cozy, with good English furniture, soft patterned fabrics, and a clock that encourages you to keep moving. However, when you are escorted into the dining room, that first impression of informality and coziness goes right out the porthole. It's dazzling, that dining room, and includes some fabulous acquisitions of royalty, gifts from other monarchs or heads of state, in the form of priceless crystal, silver, porcelains, and candelabra.

That is not all there is to the floating palace atmosphere. Twelve members of the Royal Marine Band are aboard, done up in their best red uniforms. They play from cocktail time on, right through the Royal dinner, and they close official parties by beating the retreat. On *Britannia*, although dress is extremely informal in the daytime, one dresses for dinner every night. It is lovely, lovely indeed, to sip a dry martini while awaiting Her Majesty, tapping your foot as the red-coated Royal Marines play "I've Grown Accustomed to Her Face."

Dinner is at eight, and when at sea the palace chef puts out good, straightforward food. The Queen has pushed enough rich dishes aside, in her reigning years, to sink a battleship. On *her* yacht the food is ample and simple. Meat or fish is the main course, and there are plenty of potatoes and vegetables. There is no salad course, but cheese is served and there is bread fresh from the oven. Inevitably the chef produces a fattening dessert.

Plenty of wine is served. Coffee is brought to the drawing room afterwards. On traveling nights at sea the dining room is cleared and used as a movie theatre, and crew members are always invited to watch the films.

There is a sweet informality about life aboard. A second drink is permissible, if you like, before dinner, and so is a nightcap or two after. One noticeable departure from royal custom is that any members of the group can tootle off to bed before the Queen does if they want to. "With your permission, Ma'am?" "Of course, Algernon, sleep well," Her Majesty says, smiling but vague, paying attention only to the next Scrabble word. Deck tennis is the favored sport and a canvas swimming pool is put up aft when warm weather prevails, but the Queen takes part in neither sport. You don't see the Queen in a bathing suit, or wielding a deck tennis racquet. She stays at her desk, working at Monarchy.

Her wardrobe is so carefully planned that it is charted on the wall of her dressing room. This bag goes with that hat, and those gloves with this dress. If this is Bangkok, it must be the blue printed silk. She *does* wear her clothes more than once, indeed she does. Norman Hartnell has designed the major portion of the Queen's wardrobe for many, many years. His designs throw no fear into the heart of an Yves St. Laurent, but the Yves St. Laurent ladies have none of the problems that the Queen of England has. No one does. Royal dignity is always a booby trap. Remember Grace Kelly arriving in Monte Carlo, just before she became Princess Grace, wearing that ridiculous, huge white organdy sombrero? The Queen would have nixed that one instantly if Norman Hartnell had even dared propose it.

When *Britannia* is at sea, there are no long lazy days for "Herself," as the Queen is referred to by those

184

close to her, although she is apparently unaware of her nickname. "Herself's" work comes to her aboard *"Brit,"* which is the yacht's nickname. Bags and boxes are brought aboard in every port, and there is daily helicopter delivery when *"Brit"* is within range. English newspapers, new books, magazines, and journals arrive along with the official mail and official worries.

On a long royal tour the Queen usually flies to join *Britannia* in some far-flung port; or if she has started out on *"Brit,"* she will then fly home. A round trip of three or four months aboard takes up too much of her time.

At least ten members of the press are assigned to cover the royal tours. These press members cannot have skin, they must have the hide of a rhinoceros. It's a scramble for them, from start to finish. They have to arrive before the Queen in every port, and leave after her. Months of hop, skip, and jump make all of them long for those dear old hammocks of the old days. The Queen works long hours, but at least she can put her feet up and order caviar when she returns to her sea palace. Gentlemen of the press, assigned to glorify her, keep to a schedule that would daunt an albatross.

The publicizing of monarchy is extremely clever, and it is here that *Britannia* is even a bigger star than the Queen. By and large, royal tours are dull and uneventful, with the same smiles on the same faces in the same places. Reporters and photographers pray for a little fun somewhere along the line. In Singapore a fine white elephant sat down and absolutely refused to get up to be presented to the Queen, and that story became headline stuff. "Elephant Refuses to Curtsey to Queen," it was headed. Anything for a laugh. Or a smile. Photographers watch zealously for Elizabeth II's smile. It has lit up newspapers and magazines for a quarter of a century now, and is one of the most interesting things that she does. Photographically, that is.

§

The effect made by *Britannia* and the Queen is staggering, no matter where they go. On one of the tours, the Queen

and Prince Philip spent several days in the Seychelle islands. The Seychelle islands are a last, lost paradise, deep
in the heart of the Indian Ocean, and have been a British
Crown Colony for over 150 years, although no British mon-
arch had ever set foot there until March 1972, when the
Queen and *Britannia* appeared.

The Queen and spring arrived in the Seychelles at
approximately the same time. The Queen, with proper
royal prerogative, arrived a little bit earlier. *Britannia* appeared off Cousine, a tiny island that is also a bird sanc-
tuary that Prince Philip had visited a few years before on
behalf of his World Wildlife interests. He remembered the
endless beaches, the total privacy, and the strange exotic
birds. By now, the tour had lasted for six weeks and the
Queen was exhausted from working and smiling her way
through the killing temperatures of Thailand, Malaysia,
and Singapore.

The big blue hulk of *Britannia* dropped anchor off
Cousine early in the morning. A message had been sent to
the resident ornithologist of Cousine, who was standing by,
quite ready for the royals, and for the picnic as well. The
royal party came zooming up to the beach in a Zodiac but,
there being no dock, they had to step off the Zodiac into
waist-deep water to make it to the beach. Aside from that,
Her Majesty was every inch the Queen, although her manner of arrival shook up the warden and his wife considerably. No matter. Prince Philip barbecued fresh fish, the
Queen tossed the salad. Some of the island's rare birds, the
exquisite snow white paradise flycatchers, must have gotten some sort of royal notice, because they showed up and
showed off for everyone. It was an easy, relaxed day for all.
Unlike the next one.

At nine the next morning, *Britannia* arrived at Victoria, the capital city of the Seychelles, on the island of Mahé.
The Queen's visit had been planned for months, but no real
enthusiasm had been shown by her subjects. Instead, an odd
reticence was apparent. The Governor, Sir Bruce Greatbatch,
and the Chief Minister, James Mancham, both of whom had
met the Queen before, were excited, but the people were
showing a strange sort of lethargy. Only the schoolchildren

seemed to have made any effort. They had simple handsome gifts to present to the Queen, which was perfectly suitable since 25,000 of the 40,000 Seychelle islanders were children under fifteen. No wonder the Seychelles are known as the Isles of Love.

The houses along the Queen's route were a rainbow of turquoise and pink and yellow paint. Almost every wooden shack or house had a new coat of paint. But if you asked a resident about the Queen's visit he would look at you vaguely, and then look up at the inevitable royal picture that hangs on the wall of the poorest hut or the richest villa. To the question, "Are you excited about the Queen's visit?" the answer would be "Oh, yes," but the vague look would turn again to the picture on the wall.

It was so simple. The people of the Seychelles did not believe that the Queen of England was real. They *believed* the picture—they were used to that. But The Queen herself? There, in the poor little islands? Someone was trying to fool them.

At precisely nine A.M. on the morning of March 21, 1972, the Queen and Prince Philip boarded the royal launch, leaving *Britannia* looming behind them in the bay, and came ashore. Her Majesty wore a blue and green printed silk dress, a white straw hat with a matching ribbon and rosette band, white shoes, and she carried a white purse. Prince Philip wore a light gray suit, a striped tie, and a large grin. His hands were clasped behind his back in what has come to be known as the Prince Philip position, one that Prince Charles has copied carefully. The Queen showed a smallish smile, no more than an upturning of her lips, and she seemed as subdued as her subjects. The Governor, the Chief Minister, and all the dignitaries waited, and bowed properly when the Queen approached them. There were clusters of schoolchildren with their teachers, and a small group of subjects lined the long pier. But the crowd was practically nonexistent.

Split-second timing prevailed, as always. Appropriate remarks were exchanged quickly, then the Queen and Prince Philip walked the length of the long pier, pausing here and there to speak. The press had been shunted off in buses ahead of the royal party. It was hot and sweaty, even though it was only nine-thirty in the morning. At the main square the Queen and Prince Philip got into the Land Rover and rode, standing up for the next two miles, waving and smiling at the few curious people along the way. They transferred to the Governor's aging Austin Princess and rode to the airport, where the "swells" were all out to greet the royal party.

The Queen made a short speech, officially opening the new airport, and then moved along to the Reef Hotel, which was built with British money for British tourists. From there, her route led over the mountains and around the island, where she would stop at several schools, missions, and villages. The temperature soared to eighty degrees. The humidity hit one hundred.

The island grapevine had suddenly gone into full operation. The Queen really was there! The real Queen. Her big blue boat was in the harbor. The word flew. She was now at a school where the children were actually meeting her. The Queen and Prince Philip paused over and over and chatted with the children and their parents. The Queen was really there. The word flew even faster.

After lunch at the Governor's beach house, Her Majesty walked down a dusty lane in the blazing sun to greet more of her subjects. The heat was stultifying by now, but the Queen was game. The island population had finally shaken off their disbelief and lethargy, and they were turning out by the thousands. Somehow, they knew exactly where she would be every moment. Now, even the noises changed. Where there had been polite silence or polite whispers up until then, the air was full of excited voices and laughter. The Queen! Suddenly the Queen is here!

By two-thirty in the afternoon there was not one living soul on the island of Mahé who did not know where their Queen was, and every single one of them set out to see her. They all knew that she was at the mission and would soon be coming over the mountain pass, back into Victoria. She was going to go aboard her huge blue yacht and change clothes, and then she was coming ashore for a garden party given for her by the Governor. Members of the crew of her yacht were ashore already, playing soccer with the Victoria team and being soundly beaten. Tonight there was a block party in the town square. The Queen and Prince Philip were giving a party aboard *Britannia* for the upper crust, and the word was out that she had brought a present for the islanders.

By the time her car came over the top of the pink granite mountains and down into the city of Victoria, the roads were lined solid. The Seychellois have little in the way of material possessions, but they do have the biggest whitest teeth in the world. Thousands of shy but toothy grins turned toward the Queen's shy smile.

She boarded *Britannia*, changed into a yellow silk print dress, and came ashore for the Governor's garden party. The entire population of Mahé was either at the long pier or lining the road up to the Governor's mansion, and the atmosphere was one of sheer ecstasy.

At six o'clock Her Majesty herself attended retreat in the main square. The light was fading, but not the Queen. A fourteen-hour day is normal for her. When she boarded the launch to return to *Britannia*, her smile was really aglow. She had been unusually touched by the naïveté of the children and the gentle people of the Seychelles. She understood well the effect of her presence. It is frequently overwhelming.

The effect of *Britannia*, now ablaze with strings of lights, was equally overwhelming. The Queen had come to visit and had brought her palace with her, and tonight she was giving a party aboard. If she had flown, none of this could have happened. During the afternoon, the ship's doctor had come ashore and shown the local hospital staff how to use the X-ray equipment that had been brought from Britain in the yacht. Crate after crate of school books had been delivered to numerous schools on the island. But there was still a surprise present to come.

The royal launch and several other of "Brit's" boats were used to carry invited guests out to *Britannia* at seven in the evening. That night, once the guests were aboard, friendly and polite voices greeted each of them, putting them at ease and directing them toward the anteroom where the Queen was receiving. The Royal Marine Band was playing "Born Free." The floating palace was lit up like the aurora borealis and a super-civilized, polite atmosphere prevailed. It gave way to grandeur as "Herself" came face to face with her subjects. She was wearing a pale pink silk evening gown with ribbons and decorations galore. Diamonds shone from her tiara as well as from her fingers, ears, and bosom. She stood in the anteroom with Prince Philip and greeted everyone with a personal remark and the warm smile that by now had become so familiar. Drinks were served in the drawing room. Again, that deceptively informal atmosphere prevailed. But it changed, as always, when the dining room doors were opened.

The buffet was so sumptuous you would have thought the host was Henry the Eighth, not Elizabeth the Second. The menu was reminiscent of home. The Queen and her royal chef have found that good old roast beef and Yorkshire pudding bring a homesick gleam to British eyes, so they are always included, even though they are hidden behind the chef's more dramatic culinary artistry. The chef's display is for effect as well as for sustenance. The footmen and pages from Buckingham Palace were, as always, perfectly solicitous of the guests. The Royal Marine Band was playing "On the Street Where You Live."

The Queen's last present to her islanders was the best of all. She had brought them fireworks. The X-ray machine was helpful and the books were vital, but the islanders had never seen fireworks before. The Queen shot the works for the first fireworks display ever in her Indian Ocean islands. A group of Royal Navy men, highly trained in special effects, had been at work on a nearby point of land all afternoon setting up the display. Nothing the south of France has ever seen could hold a Roman candle to the Queen's display.

Ashore, the islanders were having the best party they had ever had in their lives, dancing in the streets, toasting the Queen, and oh'ing and ah'ing at lit-up *Britannia* sitting out there in the bay with their Queen aboard. When the fireworks went off, it was the star on top of the Christmas tree.

At eleven o'clock on the dot, the Royal Marine Band beat the retreat aboard *"Brit."* Guests immediately did the same. Each lady and gentleman took a last, lingering look at the Queen and Prince Philip as they boarded the launches. Once ashore, most of them joined the party in the town square and danced the rest of the night away.

The great blue hulk of *Britannia*, with her strings of lights glowing like stars in the Indian Ocean skies, remained offshore in the bay. At midnight she began to move slowly away. From the long pier, from the town square, and from the high hills and mountain homes of Mahé, every island eye watched as *Britannia* moved majestically out to sea. In a very short time all that could be seen was the last of her lights, leaving a faint glow in the dark. And the memory of a Dream and a Queen, and a Floating Palace.